PECT
Special Education PreK-8
SECRETS

Study Guide
Your Key to Exam Success

PECT Test Review for the
Pennsylvania Educator Certification Tests

Dear Future Exam Success Story:

Congratulations on your purchase of our study guide. Our goal in writing our study guide was to cover the content on the test, as well as provide insight into typical test taking mistakes and how to overcome them.

Standardized tests are a key component of being successful, which only increases the importance of doing well in the high-pressure high-stakes environment of test day. How well you do on this test will have a significant impact on your future, and we have the research and practical advice to help you execute on test day.

The product you're reading now is designed to exploit weaknesses in the test itself, and help you avoid the most common errors test takers frequently make.

How to use this study guide

We don't want to waste your time. Our study guide is fast-paced and fluff-free. We suggest going through it a number of times, as repetition is an important part of learning new information and concepts.

First, read through the study guide completely to get a feel for the content and organization. Read the general success strategies first, and then proceed to the content sections. Each tip has been carefully selected for its effectiveness.

Second, read through the study guide again, and take notes in the margins and highlight those sections where you may have a particular weakness.

Finally, bring the manual with you on test day and study it before the exam begins.

Your success is our success

We would be delighted to hear about your success. Send us an email and tell us your story. Thanks for your business and we wish you continued success.

Sincerely,

Mometrix Test Preparation Team

Need more help? Check out our flashcards at: http://MometrixFlashcards.com/PECT

TABLE OF CONTENTS

Top 20 Test Taking Tips....1
Foundations and Professional Practice....2
Understanding Students with Disabilities....27
Assessment and Program Planning and Implementation....53
Inclusive Learning Environments....62
Delivery of Specially Designed Instruction....80
Practice Test....90
- Practice Questions....90
- Answers and Explanations....107

Secret Key #1 - Time is Your Greatest Enemy....116
- Pace Yourself....116

Secret Key #2 - Guessing is not Guesswork....116
- Monkeys Take the Test....116
- $5 Challenge....117

Secret Key #3 - Practice Smarter, Not Harder....118
- Success Strategy....118

Secret Key #4 - Prepare, Don't Procrastinate....118
Secret Key #5 - Test Yourself....119
General Strategies....119
Special Report: How to Overcome Test Anxiety....125
- Lack of Preparation....125
- Physical Signals....126
- Nervousness....126
- Study Steps....128
- Helpful Techniques....129

Special Report: Additional Bonus Material....134

Top 20 Test Taking Tips

1. Carefully follow all the test registration procedures
2. Know the test directions, duration, topics, question types, how many questions
3. Setup a flexible study schedule at least 3-4 weeks before test day
4. Study during the time of day you are most alert, relaxed, and stress free
5. Maximize your learning style; visual learner use visual study aids, auditory learner use auditory study aids
6. Focus on your weakest knowledge base
7. Find a study partner to review with and help clarify questions
8. Practice, practice, practice
9. Get a good night's sleep; don't try to cram the night before the test
10. Eat a well balanced meal
11. Know the exact physical location of the testing site; drive the route to the site prior to test day
12. Bring a set of ear plugs; the testing center could be noisy
13. Wear comfortable, loose fitting, layered clothing to the testing center; prepare for it to be either cold or hot during the test
14. Bring at least 2 current forms of ID to the testing center
15. Arrive to the test early; be prepared to wait and be patient
16. Eliminate the obviously wrong answer choices, then guess the first remaining choice
17. Pace yourself; don't rush, but keep working and move on if you get stuck
18. Maintain a positive attitude even if the test is going poorly
19. Keep your first answer unless you are positive it is wrong
20. Check your work, don't make a careless mistake

Foundations and Professional Practice

Professional collaboration

Although practitioners of infant and toddler caregiving may not refer to a part of their work as curriculum planning, they nevertheless do fulfill this function. They do this by identifying the experiences and routines that will nurture children's development and learning and enable children to reach the identified developmental and learning goals and then developing plans for systematically providing children with these experiences and routines. Early childhood and preschool education teachers do not work in isolation. Instead, they collaborate with caregivers and teachers working with children younger than their own students and with teachers working with students in higher grades than theirs. Caregivers and teachers share information about individual children as they progress through grade levels, about groups and classes, and about general developmental levels and transitions. They collaboratively strive to achieve greater continuity and connection across age and grade levels, at the same time preserving the appropriateness and integrity of instructional practices within each level.

Resources available for professional development and learning

- Professional literature - books and publications are examples of literature that can help a classroom teacher.
- Colleagues - a fellow member of a profession, staff, or academic faculty; an associate
- Professional Associations - an association of practitioners of a given profession, for example NEA, NSTA, etc.
- Professional development activities – sometimes put on by a local or state school board to teach educators the newest trends in education.

Code of Ethics

Ethical codes are specialized and specific rules of ethics. Such codes exist in most professions to guide interactions between specialists with advanced knowledge, e.g., doctors, lawyers and engineers, and the general public. They are often not part of any more general theory of ethics but accepted as pragmatic necessities. Ethical codes are distinct from moral codes that apply to the education and religion of a whole larger society. Not only are they more specialized, but they are more internally consistent, and typically can be applied without a great deal of interpretation by an ordinary practitioner of the specialty.

School as a resource to the larger community

Our mission is to work with communities to ensure learner success and stronger communities through family-school-community partnerships. Through schools, individuals value learning; learn how to learn; demonstrate effective communication, thinking and problem solving; enjoy a better quality of life; are fulfilled; experience the joy of learning; and contribute to and benefit from the intergenerational transmission of culture. in supporting the educational role and function of local education agencies (and organizations), families, and communities increase local capacity to improve and ensure learning opportunities for the children and citizens of the community.

Advocating for learners

Public support for education is fragile. Poverty jeopardizes the well-being and education of our young people and some communities are caught in a downward spiral of cynicism and mistrust. Teachers must necessarily be advocates for education. One might become involved in efforts to change policies, programs, and perceptions to benefit learners; such involvement is crucial for educators today, for when they do not create effective channels of communication with legislators, the media, and community members, their opinions will very likely go unfulfilled legislatively. These consequences can be devastating to children and to learning. The stakes are simply too high for educators not to engage in advocacy efforts. Just as teaching and learning require commitment, energy, and perseverance, so too does advocacy.

Parental education

As families shrank during the last half of the past century, parental education rose. Among adolescents ages 12-17 in 1940, about 70% had parents who had completed no more than 8 years of school, while only 15% had parents who were high school graduates, and 3% had parents who were college graduates. Expenditures for education have expanded enormously since then, and the educational attainment figures have been turned on their head. By 2000, only 6% of adolescents ages 12-17 have parents with no more than 8 years of school, while 82% have parents with high school diplomas, including the 21%-29% who have mothers or fathers with 4-year college degrees.

Parental educational attainment is perhaps the most central feature of family circumstances relevant to overall child well-being and development, regardless of race/ethnicity or immigrant origins. Parents who have completed fewer years of schooling may be less able to help their children with schoolwork because of their limited exposure to knowledge taught in the classroom. They also may be less able to foster their children's educational success in other ways because they lack familiarity with how to negotiate educational institutions successfully. Children whose parents have extremely limited education may, therefore, be more likely to benefit from, or to require, specialized educational program initiatives if their needs are to be met by educational institutions.

Parents with limited educational attainment may also be less familiar with how to access successfully social institutions, such as healthcare, with which children and their parents must interact in order to receive needed services. Equally important is that parent educational attainment influences their income levels. Parents with limited education tend to command lower wages in the labor market and are, therefore, constrained in the educational, health, and other resources that they can afford to purchase for their children. For all of these reasons, among children generally, negative educational and employment outcomes have been found for children with low parental educational attainment.

Student diversity

Cultural identities are strongly embraced by adolescents but they also want to be recognized and treated as unique individuals. Teachers walk a fine line between respecting cultural differences and avoiding overly emphasizing them or disregarding them altogether. Responding to discriminatory comments immediately, using a wide variety of examples, quoting scholars from many cultures and identifying universal problems needing complex solutions can indirectly communicate appreciation of and respect for all cultures. Teachers must take care never to imply any kind of stereotype or make comments that might indicate a cultural bias. They must refrain from asking a student to respond as a member of a particular culture, class or country. Teachers should learn as much as they can about every racial, ethnic and cultural group represented in their classroom. It is also important that teachers respect students' commitments and obligations away from school, their family responsibilities and job pressures.

Cultural influences

Study after study has shown that a student's culture has a direct impact on learning. Since educational standards are based on white, middle class cultural identification, students who do not fall into that demographic face challenges every day. It's not that these students are incapable of learning; they simply judge that which is important and how they express that importance differently. Sometimes it is difficult for them to understand and relate to curriculum content, teaching methods and social skills required because their culture does things differently, emphasizes different choices and rewards different behavior. Adolescents identify with their culture; they become what they know. If teachers ignore cultural differences, it causes communication issues, inhibits learning and increases the potential for behavior problems. As long as a child has no physical or mental health issues, he is capable of learning. He simply needs that the information presented and examples used to be relevant to his life experiences; otherwise, it does not seem to make sense to him.

Social environment

The social environment is the set of people and institutions with which one associates and communicates. It has both a direct and indirect influence on behavior by the individuals within the group. It is sometimes defined by specific characteristics such as race, gender, age, culture or behavioral patterns. When defined by behavioral patterns it can lead to unproven assumptions about entire groups of people. In America's diverse society, it is essential that teachers recognize that various social groups exist within a classroom and thus determine the best strategies not only to facilitate the learning of "book" facts, but also to encourage understanding and acceptance between the groups. The learning theory called social cognitivism believes that people learn by observing others, whether they are aware of the process or not. Creating opportunities for students to interact with diverse social groups in a neutral, non-threatening situation can bring about positive interpersonal growth that could have long-term societal impact outside of the educational environment.

Socialization

Socialization is the process of learning the written and unwritten rules, acceptable behavioral patterns, and accumulated knowledge of the community in order to function within its culture. It is a gradual process that starts when a person is born and, in one form or another, continues throughout his life. There are many "communities" within a culture: e.g., family, school, neighborhood, military and country. There are six forms of socialization:
- Reverse Socialization: deviation from acceptable behavior patterns.
- Developmental Socialization: the process of learning social skills.
- Primary Socialization: learning the attitudes, values and actions of a culture.

- Secondary Socialization: learning behavior required in a smaller group within the culture.
- Anticipatory Socialization: practicing behavior in preparation for joining a group.
- Resocialization: discarding old behavior and learning new behavior as part of a life transition; e.g., starting school, moving to a new neighborhood or joining the military.

The agents of socialization are the people, groups and institutions that influence the self-esteem, emotions, attitudes, behavior and acceptance of a person within his environment. The first agents are the immediate family (mother, father, siblings) and extended family (grandparents, aunts, uncles, cousins). They influence religious affiliation, political inclinations, educational choices, career aspirations and other life goals. The school's role is explaining societal values, reinforcing acceptable behavior patterns and teaching necessary skills such as reading, writing, reasoning and critical thinking. Peer groups (people who are about the same age) share certain characteristics (attend the same school, live in the same neighborhood) and influence values, attitudes and behavior. The media (radio, television, newspapers, magazines, the Internet) have an impact on attitude, values and one's understanding of the activities of society and international events. Other institutions that influence people include religion, the work place, the neighborhood, and city, state and federal governments.

Social ineptitude

Social ineptitude is defined as a lack of social skills; in most societies, this term is considered disrespectful. There are medical conditions that may cause a deficiency in social skills such as autism and Asperger syndrome. Someone who believes himself socially inept may have an avoidant personality disorder. A shy person or an overly bold person may observe societal conventions but still exhibit social incompetence; the behavior is simply manifested in different ways. The criteria for social ineptitude are different in different cultures, which makes it difficult to cite specific examples. People trying to integrate into a new environment may unknowingly commit a social faux pas thereby earning the damaging label unfairly. In a culturally diverse classroom, it is critical to create an atmosphere of acceptance so if a student does something inappropriate, the behavior can be quietly and gently corrected without causing humiliation or embarrassment.

Social skills

Social skills are the tools used to interact and communicate with others. They are learned during the socialization process and are both verbal and non-verbal. These skills are integral to becoming an active and accepted member of any environment. There are general skills needed to complete daily transactions such as being able to ask sensible questions and provide logical answers and knowing how to read and write and understand simple directions. If these skills are missing or poorly executed, it can cause various problems and misunderstandings, some of which could have long-lasting and/or life-changing consequences. In smaller groups, other skills may be needed such as the ability to engage in interesting conversation, present ideas to peers, teach new concepts or actively participate in discussions. Using body language and gestures appropriate to the situation and the message, having the ability to resolve conflicts and being diplomatic when necessary are examples of advanced social skills.

Meeting with parents

Studies have shown that the more parents are involved in their children's education, the better the students learn and the fewer behavior problems one must handle. Teachers are an integral part of the process. It is up to them to keep parents informed about the academic and social progress of the students. Report cards only provide letter or number grades and are not designed to explore and explain how well the student is learning and progressing in the intangible skills like critical thinking, reasoning ability, study habits, attitude, communication with adults and peers and other social and interactive development. Sending home periodic progress reports is an effective way to keep parents abreast of changes. Meeting with parents regularly to discuss their child's particular progress and being available to answer questions are excellent ways to work together as a team to ensure the student benefits the most from his educational experience.

Parent/student/teacher agreement

If a teacher should wish to use a formal parent/student/teacher agreement as a way to involve parents, provide students with a written set of expectations and explain their commitment to a successful educational experience, there are several activities that can be included:
- Parent Priorities:
  - Show respect for and support of the student, teacher and the discipline policy.
  - Monitor homework assignments and projects.
  - Attend teacher conferences.
  - Ask about the student's day.
- Student Priorities:
  - Show respect for parents, teachers, peers and school property.
  - Put forth his best effort both in class and at home.
  - Come to class prepared.
  - Talk to his parents about school.
- Teacher Priorities:
  - Show respect for the student, his family and his culture.
  - Help each student strive to reach his potential.
  - Provide fair progress evaluations to students and parents.
  - Enforce rules fairly and consistently.

Many schools use some sort of parent/student/teacher agreement to ensure everyone understands the rules and agrees to abide by them. It can be as simple as requiring parents, students and teachers to sign a copy of the student handbook or it can be a formal contract drafted with specific activities each pledges to perform. Whichever format is used, it should detail each party's responsibilities. This accomplishes several goals:
- Parents are recognized as an important part of the educational experience. They are also made aware of what is expected of them, their children, the teachers and the administration.
- Students are given written expectations, which prevent an "I didn't know" attitude. It encourages respect for himself, his parents, his teachers, his peers and the rules.

- Teachers make a written commitment to students and parents to provide an environment that encourages learning. They list specific, observable behavior which they pledge to perform.

Levels of parental involvement

Some parents are eager to participate in their child's education, some do so only when required, and others avoid involvement of any kind. All three approaches can be a challenge. Eager parents may bombard the teacher and administration with notes, phone calls, emails and requests for information and meetings. Setting reasonable, well-defined limits may be necessary. Parents who only show up when specifically requested (e.g., semi-annual parent/teacher conferences, meeting with the administration about a behavior problem), might only be going through the motions in order to keep their child enrolled in school. They may be incapable of or don't really care to address any underlying issues; they show up because they are required to do so. Parents who are never available and impossible to contact provide no help or insight and offer no support.

Parent/teacher conferences

Basics
Parent/teacher conferences can be stressful experiences for both parties. But with a positive attitude and much preparation, they can be pleasant, provide a forum for the exchange of information and improve the educational experience for the students. The first step is for the teacher to be rested. Fatigue can cause an inability to concentrate, unfortunate misunderstandings and inappropriate reactions. If a teacher thinks parents might be difficult to handle, it might be wise to ask an administrator to sit in. The teacher needs to have a plan prepared with discussion points and copies of the student's work available to review. He needs to keep in mind that the parents may have items to discuss as well, and therefore the plan needs to be flexible and allow time for questions. The discussion should focus on the positive and present negative information with a "we can fix it" approach.

In order to avoid wasting everyone's time during a parent/teacher conference, there are several things a teacher can do to set the scene for a productive meeting. Make initial contact early by sending a note or newsletter home briefly outlining plans and objectives for the year and providing contact information (e.g., phone number, email address, days and times available). This tells parents the teacher is willing to talk and/or meet when necessary. When a date for a conference is set, the teacher should be certain to invite both parents. It is the best way to gauge how involved they are, yet individual family circumstances need to be considered (one-parent families, parents' work commitments, et cetera). Schedule twenty to thirty minute conferences; if more time becomes necessary, schedule a follow-up meeting. Develop a flexible agenda and gather necessary paperwork. Verify parent and student names just before the meeting.

Encouraging parental involvement
Every teacher needs to develop ways in which to involve parents in the education of their children. Some communication methods may be more effective than others depending upon the age of the students, the educational level and time limitations of the parents, and the administrative support and resources available to the teacher. Some schools encourage a parent orientation program at the beginning of the year, in which the teacher informs

parents what his expectations are concerning behavior and outlines classroom rules. He presents a broad picture of the material to be covered, projects that will be assigned and homework requirements. If a meeting isn't possible, the same information can be conveyed in a letter sent home just before school starts or during the first week. Besides regularly scheduled parent/teacher conferences, a periodic newsletter, perhaps when report cards are issued, can be sent to update parents.

Being prepared

Parent/teacher conferences are the best time for candid communication. For the encounter to be productive, both parties need to be prepared to discuss the student's strengths and weaknesses, share any concerns and decide upon the best way to help the student meet required goals and reach his potential. Some topics to consider in preparation for this important meeting:

- The skills and knowledge that should be learned and mastered.
- Required academic standards. Give parents a copy to which to refer during the year, and explain these standards.Projects planned and assignments required to complete academic requirements.The evaluation method, what data is considered and when progress reports are issued.How parents can help. Suggest concrete activities which they can do at home in order to encourage learning and support the teacher's efforts.Programs available for both fast and slow learners.What programs are available to prepare students for life after high school.

Things to remember

Try to use a table rather than a desk and chairs so that the parents and the teacher meet as equals; this creates a more relaxed environment. Start with a positive statement about the student and then briefly review the objectives of the meeting. The teacher should not do all of the talking; it should be a conversation, not a monologue. Avoid educational jargon. Many parents will not understand it or will interpret it incorrectly. Focus on strengths, give specific examples, provide suggestions for improvement and refer to actions rather than character. For example: "Sam turned in his essay the day after it was due," instead of "Sam is irresponsible." Ask for parents' opinions and listen to their responses. Use body language that shows interest and concern and make eye contact. Do not judge the parents' attitude or behavior, and consider cultural differences. Briefly summarize the discussion and end with a positive comment or observation about the student.

Conclusion

If either the teacher or the parents feel that there is more to discuss or that a follow-up meeting is necessary for an update on progress made, a time can be scheduled before the parents leave. As soon as possible after the conversation while the details are fresh, the teacher should make notes of the general discussion and record any specific actions that he or the parents agreed to take as well as the parents' attitude and willingness to offer support. Any private information and/or family issues which the parents shared should be kept in the strictest confidence. If a cooperative relationship is to be established, parents need to know that their family business will remain private. It is very important and even required in some states that teachers report any indication of or concerns about possible child abuse or endangerment to the authorities. All teachers and administrators need to be familiar with the pertinent statutes in their state.

Cooperating with colleagues

To be successful, a teacher must be constantly cooperating with and learning from colleagues. There are a number of ways to do this; one is to set up regular meetings with them. Many teachers are part of a team of teachers who instruct the same group of students, and these meetings will therefore already be in place. If this is not the case, however, teachers should try to set up frequent meetings with colleagues who either teach the same students or the same subject. These meetings should not be the equivalent of teacher's lounge gripe sessions, but instead should be forums in which new teaching methods can be discussed, teaching content can be coordinated, and basic plans of behavior management can be established.

Peer review programs for teachers

Another way in which a community of teachers can foster professional improvement is through peer review. In a peer review program, teachers observe one another and offer suggestions for improvement. This is especially helpful when it is done among teachers in the same grade level or subject. Another teacher who is fluent in French, for instance, would be a great resource for a non-French-speaking teacher helping new immigrants from West Africa. Of course, in order for this sort of program to work, there needs to be a spirit of collaboration and constructive criticism among the teachers. Unfortunately, school politics and competitiveness often poison the relationships between colleagues, and make it difficult to offer or accept well-meaning suggestions. The best peer review programs establish a specific protocol for criticism and encouragement.

Mentoring programs for teachers

Mentoring is another professional improvement program that can be extremely valuable to a teacher. In a mentoring program, experienced teachers develop relationships with beginning teachers. The schools that use these programs find that they are able to retain a larger proportion of their beginning teachers. When mentoring programs are not offered, new teachers should ask a veteran teacher to act as a mentor, as a mentor can provide guidance on any aspect of teaching, from classroom management to lesson plans. New teachers get the most out of the relationship if they consciously remain open to constructive criticism. A mentor should observe his or her mentee directly in the teacher's classroom, but the mentee should also keep a list of concerns and questions to bring to private meetings. Teachers who accept advice and are willing to see things from a different perspective will grow immeasurably from the mentoring experience.

Peer tutoring programs

Another way that teachers can join with their colleagues in order to improve the quality of instruction is through peer tutoring. In a basic peer tutoring program, more advanced students work with the younger students on class work. For instance, the members of a second-grade class might be paired with the members of a fifth-grade class. The older children will still be using many of the concepts that they learned in second grade, thus it will be beneficial for them to explain and demonstrate these concepts. The younger children, meanwhile, will enjoy working with older children and may be more receptive to the material when it comes from a source other than the teacher.

Peer tutoring relationships are especially fruitful when they are between students from similar backgrounds. In a modern class, there may be students from several different linguistic backgrounds. Some students may be the sole representative of their native culture in their grade level. If there are other students in the school with the same origin, however, they may be profitably united through peer tutoring. Also, peer tutoring programs are a great chance for students to develop their social skills; the older children will practice being generous and considerate of someone younger, while the younger children will practice being attentive and receptive to counsel. Of course, only those older students who have a good grasp of the content and are well-behaved should be involved in a peer tutoring program.

Field trips with other classes

Another way that teachers can band together is by arranging field trips with other teachers, as it is often easier to handle the logistics of a large field trip in cooperation with another teacher. Also, many field trips will have applications to multiple subject areas. For instance, a trip to a local battlefield could have relevance for American history, English, and Social Studies students. A visit to the local natural science museum could be pertinent to content in math, science, and history. It is always a good idea to encourage students to make associations between content areas. Furthermore, a field trip encourages students to mix with other students, forming social connections that improve investment in the academic setting.

Coordinating subject matter

One of the most positive ways for teachers to work with their fellow teachers is by coordinating subject matter. This strategy is often used in teacher "teams" in elementary and middle school, but it can also be effective in high school. Let us consider a brief example of how teachers can coordinate subject matter with great results. Imagine that you are a sixth-grade teacher. Before the school year begins, you could propose that the sixth grade uses "cities" as a theme. Each teacher can then construct lessons in their instructional domain that connect with this theme. As the teacher, you could look at texts that focus on life in the city. The history teacher could teach students about the rise of the big urban centers during the Industrial Revolution. The math teacher could incorporate some study of the various statistics and charts that are used to describe and learn about cities. If your school is located in or near a large city, you might also take some field trips so students can observe first-hand the things that they have learned.

Coordinating instructional content

The net effect of coordinating content seems to be that students learn more. Educational research suggests that all knowledge is associative, and people therefore tend to remember those things that they can easily fit into their existing store of information. If a teacher and his colleagues can link diverse disciplines together by looking at the same subject from a number of different perspectives, they can help students develop a well-rounded and coherent way of intellectually exploring the world. This is especially true for students, who will be encountering a dizzying amount of new information at school. If this material is disconnected and seemingly random, students will be more likely to forget it. Thematic content in multiple subjects helps avoid this problem.

Communicating with colleagues

An instructor should meet with his colleagues at some point during the year so that he can get a general idea of the structure and content of his colleague's classes. During the year, the teacher should stay abreast of that which students are learning in their other classes, and should note associations between disciplines whenever they arise. A teacher should also know when his fellow teachers are assigning major projects or exams, so that he can avoid giving important assignments on the same day. Many schools assign a certain day of the week for tests in each subject; e.g., math tests on Monday, history tests on Tuesday, and so on. If the school does not do this, the teacher should make sure that major projects and examinations are scheduled such that students are not overwhelmed with a flurry of work.

Relationship with school administration

It is important for the teacher to have a strong relationship with the school administration. The principals and support staff of a school are supposed to be there to make life easier, but they can only do this with cooperation. In order to maintain a happy partnership with the school administration, teachers should remember one guideline of great importance: namely, teachers should always report any significant problems immediately; these problems can include disciplinary matters, personal problems, or conflict with school protocol. In large schools where there is little one-on-one contact between the administration and the faculty, it is common for teachers to let their grievances fester in silence. The result is that what could be a cooperative relationship becomes poisoned by resentment and frustration. Teachers who have complaints or concerns about the way the school is being run, or who need help, should immediately discuss the problem with the principal.

Meeting with the principal

A teacher should try to avoid only visiting the principal when there is something wrong. A principal, like any person, will develop certain assumptions about a teacher whom they only see in times of crisis. Also, many principals will resent those teachers who they feel are constantly passing their problems onto the administration. Teachers should be referring problems to the principal only as a last resort. It is appropriate to let the principal know about concerns without necessarily asking for help. A teacher should try to check in with the principal periodically when things are going well in class, so that he or she can get a more balanced appreciation of the class' progress. When a teacher maintains a good relationship with the principal throughout the year, he or she will be much more helpful on those occasions of crisis.

Scheduling an observation by the principal

One great way to cultivate a positive relationship with the principal is to invite him or her to sit in on a class. A teacher should invite the principal on a day when a particularly innovative and exciting lesson is planned. It is a good idea to let the students know ahead of time that the principal will be joining the class, so they need to be on their best behavior. During the observation, the teacher should invite the principal to participate whenever appropriate. Many principals were teachers at one time, and will welcome the opportunity to join in with the activities of the class. After the class, the teacher should ask the principal for his opinion. As in relationships with other teachers, teachers should try to remain open to criticism and accepting of advice. These kinds of observations can be very useful for beginning teachers, who may be unaware of some fundamental mistakes they are making.

Relationships with teacher aides and assistants

Some teachers are lucky enough to have full- or part-time aides and assistants. When this is the case, the teacher should make sure that the aide is being used appropriately. For the most part, an aide should not be busy doing paperwork during class time. It is certainly useful to have another person to help with grading, but this can be done during the planning period or lunch. While the children are in the classroom, the aide should be another set of eyes and ears. In other words, the aide should circulate around the room while students are working. He can answer any questions students may have about the lesson, and can make sure that students stay on-task. Aides are also useful when some members of the class have fallen behind the others. The aide can assemble those students and give them a brief refresher on the recent material as the teacher instructs the rest of the class.

Frequent updates to parents

After sending this first letter home, it is also helpful to send home periodic notes letting parents know how the class is proceeding. If one has a small number of students, one may even be able to make personal phone calls to each parent. Another way to stay in contact with many parents is through email; if one finds that all (or even some) of the parents in ones class have internet access, one may send out a short weekly update. Whatever format one chooses, one should try to keep parents informed of upcoming evaluations, field trips, and special events. If possible, one should personalize each message with some specific information about the child; this will convey the impression that one is taking a direct interest in the educational progress of each member of the class. It is important to make an effort to communicate both good news as well as bad. For many parents, the only contact they ever have with the school is when their child has gotten into trouble. One should occasionally make a call or drop a note to praise a student for improved academic performance. Parents will respond very positively to teachers who take the time to praise their children.

Keeping parents alert to student performance

It is also important to let parents know how their children are faring in class by sending home their grades regularly. Many teachers require students to take home their major tests and have them signed by a parent. Increasingly, teachers are posting student grades on a class website so that parents and students alike can keep track. Whichever method one chooses, one should make sure that one does not wait until the end of the term to let a parent know that their student is in danger of failing. As soon as any student falls behind, it is imperative to alert his parents so that a strategy for improvement can be developed. Do not assume that students will keep their parents informed as to how they are doing in class. Many students will claim to be doing well even if they know that this will be disproved by their final grade. As a teacher, it is ones responsibility to keep parents informed.

Parent-teacher conferences

Another important part of developing a positive rapport with parents is the parent-teacher conference. Most elementary schools schedule these near the beginning of the year, often at the end of the first grading period. In middle and high school, parent-teacher conferences are not always mandatory, though they are recommended. If one is a beginning teacher, one may approach ones first conferences with some anxiety. It is important to remember, however, that both the teacher and the parent both have the student's success as a goal. It is important to accurately communicate a student's standing within the class. It is also important for both parties to agree on a strategy for maintaining or improving the student's performance subsequent to the conference. Conferences are meant to be punishment for neither the instructor, the parent, nor the student.

Teacher-parent phone call

When a student is struggling, contacting his parents should not be a last resort. Rather, it should be done soon so that the student's course can be corrected. Many students act out at school because of problems they are having at home; learning about these motivating factors can not only help one understand the behavior, but can lead to possible solutions. In any case, when one calls a parent to communicate bad news, it is important to always maintain a focus on the steps that should be taken for improvement. Do not call a parent simply to gripe. At the end of the call, make plans to talk again in the near future, so that everyone can assess how the strategy for improvement is proceeding. Always treat the parent as part of a team whose aim is the success of the student.

Open house

Another traditional means of making contact with parents is the open house. Most schools hold an open house at the beginning of the year so that parents can meet the teachers and see the classrooms. Besides being an opportunity to give information about the class, the open house is a chance for the teacher to present himself in a favorable light. The neatness and organization of the room is very important, as is greeting the parents as they enter. One should try to avoid getting bogged down in discussion with any one parent; discussions of individual students should be handled in another setting. The open house is a chance for one to sell oneself and the class. One should demonstrate the structure of one's class as well as present an appeal for help from parents.

Inviting parents to class

Besides the open house, parents should be invited to school whenever their presence will have a positive impact on learning. For instance, if students are going to be putting on a group or individual presentation, parents should be invited to attend. This is especially important in elementary grades, where the presence of a parent can be extremely comforting and motivating to students. Other instances where parents could be invited to attend school are field days, class parties, and field trips. Too often, students create a rigid separation between their school and home lives. Language differences reinforce this separation. By inviting parents to class, a teacher breaks down the division between the academic and the family life, and encourages the student to incorporate what he is learning into all phases of his life.

Incorporating parents into instruction

A teacher should try to take advantage of parents' special skills or talents, especially as they relate to different content areas. For instance, if one is teaching a science-related unit and one of the students' parents is a botanist, you should invite him to speak to the class. If one is teaching a unit on Social Studies and discovers that one of the parents works for the federal government, it might be useful to invite him to speak. Whenever possible, one should be striving to make course content relevant to the daily lives of the students. There is no better way to do this than by incorporating their family members into the lesson.

Consequences of poverty

In general, poverty has been found to have negative developmental consequences for children. Children in impoverished families may be at risk of educational failure because they lack access to adequate nutrition, health care, dental care, or vision care, as well as lacking access to educational resources that parents with higher incomes can afford to purchase for their children. Children whose parents possess less education have parents who are less able to find full-time year-round work, and the work they find pays less well. As a consequence, policymakers and program administrators in areas with large numbers of children in groups with low parental education tend to have children as clients who not only have parents with limited education, but who work more sporadically, and who have limited income to provide for the needs of their children.

Respectful, reciprocal communication

One simple way to communicate more effectively is to treat the person whom you are addressing respectfully regardless of one's own emotional inclinations. Exhibiting disrespect is almost never helpful, as it immediately places the listener in an adversarial, and probably hostile frame of mind, and encourages them to disregard or dispute anything that is said. This does not mean that one has to agree with everyone and hide any opposition which one may hold to their attitudes, beliefs, values, or positions; it simply means that one should state ones differences in a way that does not belittle another's. For instance, instead of saying "that is a really stupid way of looking at the situation," it is usually more helpful to say "well, I see the situation somewhat differently." Then you can go on to explain how you see it, without ever saying directly that they are "stupid" or even wrong, but simply that it is possible to see things in different ways. Reciprocal communication involves each party receiving equal respect for their ideas and views.

Inappropriate treatment of students

According to the U.S. Children's Bureau, "More than half (approximately 53%) of all reports alleging maltreatment came from professionals, including educators, law enforcement and justice officials, medical and mental health professionals, social service professionals, and child care providers."

David Finkelhor, Director of the Crimes Against Children Research Center and Codirector of the Family Research Laboratory at the University of New Hampshire says, "The key problem is that educators are confused about what child protection does and whether it does any good." Finkelhor, who has been studying child victimization, child maltreatment, and family violence since 1977, adds, "There is the other problem that schools may not support the reporting process."

Reporting abuse

Teachers are in a unique position to observe and report suspected allegations of child abuse and neglect, but they are in a precarious position for educators - especially neophytes struggling to comprehend various community systems and the vast arena of child abuse reporting laws.

Educators should be guided by their school's internal administrative policies for reporting abuse. Sometimes, however, these polices can be confusing. Some schools, for example, encourage educators to report suspected abuse internally before contacting CPS. Nevertheless, state and federal laws mandate educators to report suspected child maltreatment-allowing school administrators to determine if a teacher's suspicions should be reported is unlawful. Because educators are not trained investigators, it is especially important for them to report suspected maltreatment and not assume the responsibility of determining whether a child has been abused.

Neglect

Neglect is the most common type of reported and substantiated maltreatment. According to the National Child Abuse and Neglect Data System, of the estimated 826,000 victims of child abuse and neglect in 1999, 58.4% - more than 482,000 children - suffered from neglect; 21.3% were physically abused, and 11.3% were victims of sexual abuse.

Whereas physical abuse tends to be episodic, neglect is more often chronic and involves inattention to a child's basic needs, such as food, clothing, shelter, medical care, and supervision. When considering the possibility of neglect, educators should look for consistencies and ask themselves such questions as:
- Does the child steal or hoard food consistently?
- Does the child consistently demonstrate disorganized thinking or unattended needs?
- Would observing the family in the context of the community provide any answers?
- Is this culturally acceptable child rearing, a different lifestyle, or true neglect?

Sexual abuse

According to CAPTA, sexual abuse is the "employment, use, persuasion, inducement, enticement, or coercion of any child to engage in, or assist any other person to engage in, any sexually explicit conduct or simulation of such conduct for the purpose of producing a visual depiction of such conduct."

Sexual abuse includes any interactions between a child and adult caretaker in which the child is used for the sexual stimulation of the perpetrator or another person. Sexual abuse may also be committed by a person under the age of 18 when that person is either significantly older than the victim or when the perpetrator is in a position of power or control over the child

Reporting child abuse

Reporting child abuse involves a complex array of dynamics. Individual subjectivity, personal perceptions, education, training, and life experiences affect everyone involved in the reporting and investigation process. To maintain objectivity, getting as many facts as possible is essential. Before calling, the reporter should have all of the important information, including the child's name, date of birth, address, telephone number, details of the suspected abuse and information about the suspected perpetrator. Are there bruises or marks? Is the child at risk if he returns home? Callers should be clear about what they are reporting. Vague statements of concern limit the screener's ability when determining whether to assign a case for investigation. Educators need enough information to answer basic questions that will be asked if they call CPS.

Behaviors that would be detrimental for an abuse case

When talking to children about suspected abuse, it's imperative not to ask leading questions or insert information. A case can easily become tainted if anyone involved asks leading questions or fills in statements for a child. The incident must be conveyed in the child's own words. Investigators, attorneys, social workers, psychologists, police detectives, and judges will scrutinize statements for information that could appear tainted if a case goes to court.

A recent study published by the American Psychological Association examined how misleading suggestions from parents influenced children's eyewitness reports. Psychologist and coauthor of the study, Debra Ann Poole, says even children as old as 7 or 8 will repeat misinformation. "Apparently," she says, "general instructions to report only what 'really happened' does not always prompt children to make the distinction between events they actually experienced versus events they only heard described by a significant adult."

Work of Special Education Teachers

Special education teachers work with children and youths who have a variety of disabilities. A small number of special education teachers work with students with intellectual disabilities or autism, primarily teaching them life skills and basic literacy. However, the majority of special education teachers work with children with mild to moderate disabilities, using the general education curriculum, or modifying it, to meet the child's individual needs. Most special education teachers instruct students at the elementary, middle, and secondary school level, although some teachers work with infants and toddlers.

What a principal needs to know about inclusion

Inclusion is the meaningful participation of students with disabilities in general education classrooms. To practice inclusion successfully the school principal and staff must understand the history, terms, and legal requirements involved as well as have the necessary levels of support and commitment. The word inclusion is not a precise term, and it is often confused with similar concepts such as least restrictive environment (LRE) and mainstreaming. Educating children in the least restrictive environment has been mandated since the 1970s, when it was a major provision of the Education for All Handicapped Children Act.

The law states that to the maximum extent appropriate, children with disabilities are educated with children who are nondisabled; and that special classes, separate schooling, or other removal of children from the regular educational environment occurs only if the nature or severity of the disability is such that education in regular classes with the use of supplemental aids and services cannot be achieved satisfactorily.

Oberti test

Court cases have produced guidelines that can be helpful in determining the best placement for a student. One of these is Oberti v. Board of Education, which specified three considerations for determining placement: (1) the steps taken by the school to try to include the child in the general education classroom; (2) the comparison between the educational benefit the child would receive in a general education classroom, including social and communication benefits, and the benefits the child would receive in a segregated classroom, and (3) possible negative effects inclusion would have on the other children in the general education class.

Behavioral disorders

Students who have emotional and behavioral disturbances exhibit significant behavioral excesses or deficits. Many labels are used to denote deviant behavior; these labels include: emotionally handicapped or disturbed, behaviorally disordered, socially maladjusted, delinquent, mentally ill, psychotic, and schizophrenic. Each of these terms refers to patterns of behavior that depart significantly from the expectations of others. In recent years, "behavioral disorders" has gained favor over "emotional disturbance" as a more accurate label leading to more objective decision-making and fewer negative connotations.

Emotionally disturbed childred

Estimates of the number of school-age children and adolescents with emotional or behavioral disorders depend on the definitions and criteria that are used. At some point in their lives, most individuals exhibit behavior that others consider excessive or inappropriate for the circumstances. Thus, frequency, intensity, duration, and context must be considered in making judgments of disturbance. Unlike some other educational disabilities, emotional and behavioral disorders are not necessarily lifelong conditions. Although teachers typically consider 10–20 percent of their students as having emotional or behavioral problems, a conservative estimate of the number whose problems are both severe and chronic is 2-3 percent of the school-age population. Currently, less than one-half that number are formally identified and receive special education services.

Disordered behavior

There is considerable agreement about general patterns or types of disordered behavior. One researcher suggests two discrete patterns that he calls "externalizers" (aggressive, disruptive, acting out) and "internalizers" (withdrawn, anxious, depressed). He identifies the following four dimensions:
- Conduct disorders (aggression, disobedience, irritability); personality Disorders (withdrawal, anxiety, physical complaints); immaturity (passivity, poor coping, preference for younger playmates); and socialized delinquency (involvement in gang subcultures).

In addition to these, other researchers discuss pervasive developmental disorders (including autism and childhood schizophrenia) and learning disorders (including attention deficit disorders with hyperactivity). Not all behaviorally disordered students experience academic difficulties, but the two factors are often associated.

- 17 -

Adapting physical education to include students with disabilities

Adapted physical education is an individualized program of developmental activities, exercises, games, rhythms and sports designed to meet the unique physical education needs of individuals with disabilities. Adapted physical education may take place in classes that range from those in regular physical education (i.e., students who are mainstreamed) to those in self contained classrooms. Although an adapted physical education program is individualized, it can be implemented in a group setting. It should be geared to each student's needs, limitations, and abilities. Whenever appropriate, students receiving an adapted physical education program should be included in regular physical education settings. Adapted physical education is an active program of physical activity rather than a sedentary alternative program. It supports the attainment of the benefits of physical activity by meeting the needs of students who might otherwise be relegated to passive experiences associated with physical education. In establishing adapted physical education programs, educators work with parents, students, teachers, administrators, and professionals in various disciplines. Adapted physical education may employ developmental, community-based, or other orientations and may use a variety of teaching styles. It takes place in schools and other agencies responsible for educating individuals.

Dual exceptionalities

Gifted students with disabling conditions remain a major group of underserved and under-stimulated youth. The focus on accommodations for their disabilities may preclude the recognition and development of their cognitive abilities. It is not unexpected, then, to find a significant discrepancy between the measured academic potential of these students and their actual performance in the classroom. In order for these children to reach their potential, it is imperative that their intellectual strengths be recognized and nurtured, at the same time as their disability is accommodated appropriately.

Children with one parent

Children with only one parent in the home tend to be somewhat disadvantaged in their educational and economic success. Children in immigrant families are much less likely than children in native-born families to have only one parent in the home, but there is substantial variation across groups. For example, no more than 10% of children live with one parent among children in immigrant families who have origins in India, Australia and New Zealand, Canada, China, and the Eastern and Southern former Soviet bloc, compared to more than 30% for those with origins in the English-speaking Caribbean, Haiti, and the Dominican Republic. Similarly, the proportion with one parent in the home is 17% to 25% for children in native-born families who are white or Asian, compared to about 50% or more for those who are Central American and mainland-origin Puerto Rican. The variation in number of parents in the household appears to be highly associated with level of parental education. For example, among children in immigrant families, only 10% live with one parent in the high education group, while 17% live with one parent in the medium and low education groups. Among children in native-born families, proportions are 18% for children with high education parents versus 49% for children with low education parents. The proportion with one parent rises from 20% at ages 0-2, to 24% at ages 3-8, and then to 25% at ages 9-13, and 26% at ages 14-17.

Having siblings

The presence of brothers and sisters in the home is a mixed blessing for most children. Siblings provide companionship, but they must share available resources. Insofar as parental time and financial resources are limited, parental resources must be spread more thinly in families with a larger number of siblings than in smaller families. Dependent siblings under age 18 are especially likely to compete for parental time and income. As a result, family size can have important consequences for the number of years of school that a child completes, and hence, for economic attainment during adulthood.

Among families of diverse native-born groups, the proportion with four or more siblings in the home ranges from 9% to 11% for Asians, Central Americans, and whites, to 18% for blacks and American Indians. In contrast, among children in immigrant families, the proportion in large families ranges more widely—from a low of 4% to 5% for children with origins in India and China, to a high of 35% for those with origins in the Pacific Islands (other than Australia and New Zealand).

As was the case with the number of parents, the number of siblings in the home also appears to be highly associated with level of parent education. Those children in families with high parental education are least likely to live with four or more siblings.

Having grandparents

Relatives, such as grandparents and older siblings, and non-relatives in the home can provide childcare or other important resources for children and families, but they may also act as a drain on family resources. Especially in families with few financial resources, doubling-up with other family or non-family members provides a means of sharing scarce resources, and benefiting from economies of scale in paying for housing, energy, food, and other consumable goods. At the same time, doubling-up can also lead to overcrowded housing conditions with negative consequences for children.
Taking grandparents, other relatives, and non-relatives together, many children have someone other than a parent or dependent sibling in the home. However, children in newcomer families are nearly twice as likely as those in native-born families to have such a person in the home. Children in white, non-Hispanic native-born or immigrant-origin families are least likely to live with such other persons.

About 9% of all children in the United States have at least one grandparent in the home, and whether or not a child lives with a grandparent is strongly correlated with racial/ethnic and immigrant status. For example, living with grandparents is much less common for white children (3%-8%) than for nonwhite children (12%-22%).

Overcrowded home

Overcrowded housing has deleterious effects on child health and well-being, including psychological health and behavioral adjustment, as well as the ability to find a place to do homework undisturbed. Nearly 1 in 5 children live in crowded housing conditions (that is, with more than one person per room). But nearly half of children in immigrant families live in overcrowded housing, compared to only 11% of children in native-born families. There is wide variation among groups, however. Among children in native-born families, the proportion in overcrowded housing ranges from 7% for whites to 40% for Native Hawaiian and other Pacific Islanders. Among children in immigrant families, the proportion in overcrowded housing among white groups is about the same as for native-born white groups, while the highest levels of overcrowding are experienced by children in immigrant families from Central America (59%) and Mexico (67%). Overcrowding is strongly correlated with parental education and poverty across racial/ethnic and immigrant generation groups, suggesting the need to double-up with relatives or non-relatives to share resources. This appears to be especially true among immigrant-origin groups. Moreover, while overcrowding improves slightly for older versus younger age groups, these reductions tend to be smaller among children in immigrant families, despite their initially higher levels.

School in need of improvement

This is the term No Child Left Behind uses to refer to schools receiving Title I funds that have not met state reading and math goals (AYP) for at least two years. If a child's school is labeled a "school in need of improvement," it receives extra help to improve and the child has the option to transfer to another public school, including a public charter school. Also, your child may be eligible to receive free tutoring and extra help with schoolwork. Contact your child's school district to find out if your child qualifies.

Caring community

A caring community is the way in which the school interacts with the surrounding neighborhood and town. In such a community, all families are welcome and the immediate area is seen in the spirit of cooperation between the students and their families. The populations of students who attend a school will tend to be diverse, and therefore all families should feel included in the community of the school. Individual students will feel included if they are treated well by the staff and their fellow students and feel that the staff has concern for their well being, and that they are valued. In order for this to work, students must feel that their input and participation is a necessary function of the school and that there is communication between all facets of the school and the community. Family and staff members work together to solve problems and the rights of all students are strictly upheld.

Constructing a caring environment in the classroom from the beginning means that insults and derogatory terms are eliminated so that students feel safe in the environment. Students should treat the teacher with courtesy and respect, and that should be reciprocated. Having interactions between students on a regular basis will increase the level of community in the classroom because students will get to know each other and not use prejudice readily. When appropriate, if the students have the chance to provide their input into that which they study, they will feel motivated to learn and share their knowledge with others. Balancing between teacher-centered and student-centered activities will spread out the activities and make students feel accountable for their own learning. Setting an appropriate way to deal with behavior will also increase the sense of community, in that students feel that they are being dealt with appropriately. This works reciprocally, as well, in that pre-set consequences for actions which are enforced fairly and regularly create a stable environment.

Zero tolerance

"Zero Tolerance" initially was defined as consistently enforced suspension and expulsion policies in response to weapons, drugs and violent acts in the school setting. Over time, however, zero tolerance has come to refer to school or district-wide policies that mandate predetermined, typically harsh consequences or punishments (such as suspension and expulsion) for a wide degree of rule violation. Most frequently, zero tolerance policies address drug, weapons, violence, smoking and school disruption in efforts to protect all students' safety and maintain a school environment that is conducive to learning. Some teachers and administrators favor zero tolerance policies because they remove difficult students from school; administrators perceive zero tolerance policies as fast-acting interventions that send a clear, consistent message that certain behaviors are not acceptable in the school.

Education law

One function of government is education, which is administered through the public school system by the Federal Department of Education. The states, however, have primary responsibility for the maintenance and operation of public schools. The Federal Government does maintain a heavy interest, however, in education. The National Institute of Education was created to improve education in the United States.

Each state is required by its state constitution to provide a school system whereby children may receive an education, and state legislatures exercise power over schools in any manner consistent with the state's constitution. Many state legislatures delegate power over the school system to a state board of education.

Compulsory attendance laws

The state of Connecticut enacted a law in 1842 which stated that no child under fifteen could be employed in any business in the state without proof of attendance in school for at least three months out of twelve. The compulsory attendance act of 1852 enacted by the state of Massachusetts included mandatory attendance for children between the ages of eight and fourteen for at least three months out of each year, of these twelve weeks at least six had to be consecutive. The exception to this attendance at a public school included: the child's attendance at another school for the same amount of time, proof that the child had already learned the subjects, poverty, or the physical or mental ability of the child to attend. The penalty for not sending your child to school was a fine not greater than $20.00 and the violators were to be prosecuted by the city. The local school committee did not have the authority to enforce the law and although the law was ineffective, it did keep the importance of school before the public and helped to form public opinion in favor of education. In 1873 the compulsory attendance law was revised. The age limit was reduced to twelve but the annual attendance was increased to twenty weeks per year. Additionally, a semblance of enforcement was established by forming jurisdictions for prosecution and the hiring of truant officers to check absences.

Governmental policies that are developmentally appropriate

ECE practitioners have crucial influences in the formation of our future citizens and democracy. As such, ethically they are responsible for practicing in accordance with professional standards. However, full implementation of these standards and practices depends upon public funds and policies that are supportive of an ECE system founded on providing all young children with high-quality, developmentally appropriate learning experiences. Educators call for progress on both sides—more developmentally appropriate practices by ECE professionals and more policies created and funds dedicated to support of these practices. Federal, state, and local policies need to reflect developmentally appropriate practice, including these at the very least: standards of early learning for young children with associated curricula and assessments; a comprehensive system governing compensation and professional development; a system for rating ECE program quality, informing families, policy makers, and the public regarding program quality, and improving program quality; coordinated, comprehensive services for young children; focus on program evaluation; and more public funding for quality, affordable programs in all settings.

Modern history and the foundations of worldwide early childhood education (ECE)

One historical source of the foundations for ECE programs was the general guidelines used in missionary programs. As programs developed, newer educational models, such as the Pestalozzi, Froebel, and Montessori models of EC learning, influenced modern approaches to emphasize individualized and group learning. Before World War II, ECE did not undergo much unifying progress. Thereafter, educators have made greater efforts toward globalized ECE unification. The postwar boom in job opportunities for women supported these efforts. In many world countries, physical care has been the main focus of ECE in most settings; some have had little access to ECE owing to funding and volunteer shortages. Age groups served, supply and demand for ECE delivery strategies, and government funding methods vary among countries. Generally, early programs did not stress educational standards. Many nations have recently made considerable efforts to secure community funding for public and private ECE. Recent research into child development and child-caregiver interaction and progress in teacher-preparation degree programs have enabled improved learning environments for young children.

Section 504, Education for the Handicapped Act (EHA), EHA amendments, and ADA

In 1973, Section 504 of the Rehabilitation Act, also called Public Law 93-112, was enacted to ensure individuals with disabilities equal access to federally financed programs and to promote their participation in them. A child must have a physical or mental impairment that substantially limits a major life activity to be eligible for a free, appropriate public education (FAPE) under Section 504. This law stimulated motivation to educate students with disabilities, contributing to the passage of the Education for All Handicapped Children Act, also called Public Law 94-142, in 1975. This law provides that all children with disabilities must receive a FAPE provided in the least restrictive environment possible and individualized. Its procedural safeguards mandate due process. The 1986's EHA amendments, or Public Law 99-457 extended special education to disabled preschoolers aged 3 to 5 years; services to infants and toddlers are at each U.S. state's discretion. And 1990's Americans with Disabilities Act (ADA) requires access for disabled people to public buildings and facilities, transportation, and communication but does not cover educational services.

Origins of the IDEA law (the Individuals with Disabilities Education Act)

Public Law 94-142, the Education for All Handicapped Children Act/Education for the Handicapped Act (EHA), passed in 1975; and Public Law 99-457, the EHA Amendments, passed in 1986, provided foundations that were expanded by new 1990 legislation. As a result, EHA was renamed the Individuals with Disabilities Education Act (IDEA). The IDEA's 6 main principles follow:
1. Publicly funded education cannot exclude any student because of the student's disability.
2. The rights of students with disabilities and of their parents are assured by the protection of due process procedures.
3. The parents of students with disabilities are encouraged to participate in their children's educations.
4. The assessment of all students must be fair and unbiased.
5. All students must be given a free, appropriate public education (FAPE), and it must be provided in the least restrictive environment (LRE) where the student and other students can learn and succeed.
6. Information related to students with disabilities and their families must be kept confidential.

U.S. federal legislation passed in 1997, 2001, and 2004 that importantly affected the education of young children with and without disabilities

The 1990 Individuals with Disabilities Education Act (IDEA) was reauthorized in 1997 and numbered Public Law 108-446. It provided more access for children with disabilities to the general education curriculum and extended collaborative opportunities for teachers, other professionals, and families of children with disabilities. No Child Left Behind (NCLB, 2001), the reauthorization of the Elementary and Secondary Education Act (ESEA), stressed accountability for outcomes by identifying schools and districts needing improvement and assuring teacher quality. It required school performance data to include disabled students' standardized test scores. NCLB emphasized giving teachers and administrators better research information and schools more resources, parents more information about their children's progress and the school's performance, and more local flexibility and control in utilizing federal education funds and in improving teacher qualifications, for example, through alternative certifications. And, 2004's IDEA reauthorization, Individuals with Disabilities Education Improvement Act (IDEIA), covers better alignment of NCLB with IDEA, appropriately identifying students needing special education, ensuring reasonable discipline while protecting special needs students defining highly qualified teachers, reducing paperwork, and increasing cooperation to decrease litigation.

Name and summarize some 20th- and 21st-century court cases where litigation led to decisions improving educational opportunities for young children.

The landmark 1998 New Jersey Supreme Court case of *Abbott v. Burke*, regarding school funding, resulted in the first court-ordered early childhood education (ECE) program. The court ordered New Jersey to establish full-day preschool programs for all 3- and 4-year-olds in disadvantaged school districts. By 2003, these programs served more than 36,000 children. In *Hoke County v. State* (2000), the North Carolina trial court ordered funding of prekindergarten programs for all 4-year-olds considered at risk. In *Montoy v. State* (2003), the District Court of Shawnee County, Kansas, found the state school funding system unconstitutional, approving Kansas educators' testimony recommending a comprehensive preschool program to be part of their state's plans to improve educational outcomes for students presenting the greatest challenges. The Arkansas Supreme Court ruled in 2002 that the state's school finance system was unconstitutional. In 2004, this court appointed 2 special masters to evaluate Arkansas compliance with that 2002 ruling. The special masters' report stated Arkansas could not offer the constitutional standard of "substantially equal educational opportunity" without providing disadvantaged children preschool programs.

States that have recently filed litigations challenging school funding

As of June 2010, the 13 U.S. states of Alaska, California, Colorado, Connecticut, Florida, Illinois, Kansas, New Jersey, North Carolina, Rhode Island, South Carolina, South Dakota, and Washington had litigations in process to challenge the constitutionality of government funding for K–12 education. They included cases that had recently been filed and cases wherein a remedy was ordered and that remedy was still in the process of being implemented. The 5 U.S. states of Delaware, Hawaii, Mississippi, Nevada, and Utah had never had a lawsuit challenging the constitutionality of school funding as of June 2010. The remaining 32 U.S. states did not currently have a lawsuit as of that date. In U.S. history, lawsuits challenging state practices of funding public schools have been brought in 45 of the 50 U.S. states.

Court litigations over school funding issues

The first court decision in educational financing litigation was in 1819 Massachusetts. In modern times, school funding cases included a 1971 California and a 1973 New Jersey case in the U.S. Supreme Court. The U.S. Supreme Court ruled in *Rodriguez v. San Antonio* (1973) that education was not a basic U.S. constitutional right; however, the plaintiffs then won their case in the Texas state courts, setting precedent for plaintiffs thereafter to use state courts and state constitutions. In the 1970s and 1980s, equity suits in Colorado, Georgia, and other states were won by defendants in about ⅔ of the cases. In Connecticut, Washington, and West Virginia, plaintiffs won some cases. But, plaintiffs have won about ⅔ of school funding decisions since 1989, including in New Hampshire and Vermont and landmark Kentucky and Montana cases, although plaintiffs lost equity cases in Maine, Nebraska, and Wisconsin. Shifting legal strategy from equity to adequacy in education increased victories. In Idaho and South Carolina, previous cases wherein defendants won were even reversed or differentiated.

A 1973 Texas case challenging the constitutionality of state school funding was taken to the U.S. Supreme Court: In *Rodriguez v. San Antonio,* the federal Supreme Court ruled that education was not a fundamental right under the U.S. Constitution. However, the plaintiffs subsequently won this after they filed it in the Texas state courts. This established a legal precedent in that later plaintiffs have directed most claims to state courts, citing the provisions of state constitutions. One strategy was to cite constitutional equal protection clauses. However, when equal protection or equity claims were unsuccessful, another strategy was to claim the right to an *adequate* education rather than an *equal* right to education under state law. When litigation failed, some have claimed state financing discrimination under Title VI of the U.S. Civil Rights Act and, in Alaska, under the post-Civil War antidiscrimination statute; however, U.S. Supreme Court rulings have recently prohibited this. Alternative strategies have included amending state constitutions, as in Florida and Oregon.

Avoiding legal and ethical problems

1. Lawful standards that EC educators can use to measure their practices include: being consistent; following the written policies and procedures; retaining objectivity and acting reasonably; documenting and reporting the facts; eschewing discrimination against protected students; and exercising due process, for example, giving parents notice of new policies, inviting their input, and observing their right to a hearing if they dispute their child's evaluation, classification, or placement.
2. EC educators should document who, what, when, and where but not why. In other words, they should stick to the facts, avoiding opinions, commentaries, and moral judgments. As is stated and practiced in Head Start programs, "If it isn't documented, it didn't happen." Simple, concise documentation is best.
3. EC teachers can write parent handbooks, staff handbooks, job descriptions, and reports of new procedures. They need not be expert writers. When EC educators write down policies and publicize them, and the readers sign them or have requested them, this constitutes giving notice.

Recent (2009) legal changes to the Americans with Disabilities Act (ADA)

The ADA Amendments Act (ADAAA, 2009) overrules prior Supreme Court decisions narrowly interpreting the ADA. This qualifies many more conditions as disabilities.
1. Physical or mental impairments substantially limiting 1 or more life activities now include immune system functioning; normal cell growth; brain, and neurological, respiratory, circulatory, endocrine, reproductive, digestive, bowel, and bladder functions, added to the existing activities of eating, sleeping, thinking, communicating, concentrating, lifting, and bending.
2. Impairments include physical (deaf, blind, or wheelchair-bound); conditions (AIDS, diabetes, or epilepsy); mental illnesses and ADHD; record of impairment, for example, cancer in remission and regarded as impaired.
3. *Reasonable accommodations* mean adaptations or modifications enabling persons with disabilities to have equal opportunities. The ADA describes this regarding equal employment opportunities, but it could also be interpreted relative to equal educational opportunities.
4. Reasonable accommodations that would cause undue hardship, for example, financial, are not required.

National Association for the Education of Young Children (NAEYC)'s Code of Ethical Conduct

The NAEYC states that it is committed to the following core values, founded in the history of early childhood care and education: the appreciation of childhood as a valuable, unique stage of human life, basing its work on knowledge of child development and learning; appreciation and support for the bonds between children and their families; the realization that children receive the best understanding and support within the context of their families, cultures (including ethnicity, racial identity, socioeconomic status, family structure, language, religious beliefs and practices, and political beliefs and views), communities, and society; showing respect for each individual's worth, dignity, and unique character, including children, their family members, and educators' colleagues; showing respect for diversity among children, their families, and educators' colleagues; and the recognition that both children and adults realize their full potentials within the contexts of relationships based upon trust and respect.

Section I, Ethical Responsibilities to Children

The first principle, taking precedence over all others, is not to harm children physically, mentally, or emotionally. Other principles address positive environments providing cognitive stimulation and supporting each child's culture, language, ethnicity, and family structure; not discriminating for or against children; involving everyone with relevant knowledge in decisions for children while protecting information confidentiality; using appropriate, multiple sources of assessment information; building individual relationships with each child, making individualized educational adaptations, and collaborating with families and specialists; familiarity with risk factors for child neglect and abuse and following state laws and community procedures protecting against these; reporting reasonable cause to suspect child abuse or neglect, following up regarding actions taken, and informing parents or guardians; assisting others suspecting child abuse or neglect in taking appropriate protective action; and being ethically responsible to protect children or inform parents or others who can protect them when becoming aware of situations or practices endangering children's safety, health, or well-being.

Understanding Students with Disabilities

Piaget's theory of cognitive development

First Stage

Piaget proposed that, from birth to 2 years of age, babies are in the sensorimotor stage, which focuses on learning through sensory input and motor output. Infants respond to information they gain about the world through their senses and discover that their motor activities can cause effects not only within themselves but also in the environment. They comprehend a sense of self and differentiate themselves from objects. They identify themselves as agents of reactions and begin to interact with their environments intentionally, for example, shaking rattles to make noise or, later, throwing bottles out of their cribs to make parents retrieve them. At around 8 to 9 months of age, babies achieve what Piaget termed object permanence: the realization that objects continue to exist even when out of sight. This realization is related to the popularity of peekaboo games with children in this age period.

Preoperational Stage

Piaget theorized that children aged from approximately 2 to 7 years progress from the sensorimotor stage of infancy to his second, preoperational stage. Piaget termed this stage *preoperational* based on his idea that children later develop the cognitive ability to perform and reverse mental operations, or use logical thought processes. He found children in the preoperational stage are not yet able to perform such operations. A key trait of this stage is egocentrism: Children cannot yet take others' viewpoints, either literally or figuratively. Piaget and colleagues conducted experiments wherein children in this age range, even after viewing objects from different sides of a table, could not predict how the objects would look to other people sitting at each side. They predicted that everybody would see the object from their own current view. Thus, in their perception, the world does revolve around egocentric children. Preoperational children learn to represent things symbolically using language and images. They also learn to classify objects by 1 property, for example, by color or shape.

Piaget characterized the thinking of preoperational children, aged roughly 2 to 7 years, as egocentric, illogical, and intuitive. He found 1 common feature of this thinking is animism that is, attributing human properties to inanimate objects. For example, a preoperational child might describe an autumn leaf falling off a tree branch as, "The tree threw that leaf away." Or a child might say, "The sun was angry at me and burned me." Another common feature of preoperational thinking is magical thinking. This thinking attributes cause-and-effect relationships where there are none. For example, children in this stage often believe their own internal thoughts or feelings cause external environmental events to occur. If they dislike or are angry at someone and secretly wish that something bad would happen, and then something bad does happen to that person, they think their wish caused it. This feature explains why young children frequently blame themselves for divorce, death, and so on, and informs parents to clarify to children that they did not cause these events.

Concrete Operations

The age ranges of Piaget's stages are approximate and can vary among individual children. Also, further research has found that, since Piaget proposed his theory, some individuals do not necessarily conform to the age ranges originally described. For example, while the approximate age range for the preoperational stage is 2 to 7 years and concrete operations begins around age 7, Piaget and others have also found children develop the concrete, operational feature of conservation of number around age 6. Conservation is recognizing a property remains the same despite differences in appearance; for example, there are 12 pennies in 1 long row but also 12 pennies arranged in 3 rows of 4 each. Conservation is 1 type of mental operation. The hallmark of concrete operations is the ability to perform mental operations and reverse them, but only using concrete objects. Abstract operations develop later in the formal operations stage, around age 11. Significantly, concrete operations coincide with beginning formal schooling and enables children to learn and use arithmetic, grammar, and so on because they can think logically.

Prenatal development

The first stage of development is the germinal period in the first 2 weeks after conception. Cells divide rapidly and begin to differentiate. Within 1 week 100 to 150 cells have formed. The zygote (fertilized egg) differentiates into layers: The innermost layer, which will become the embryo, is the blastocyst; the outermost layer of cells, which will support and nourish the embryo, is the trophoblast. Approximately 10 days following conception, the zygote becomes implanted in the uterine wall (endometrium). From 2 to 8 weeks after conception is the embryonic period. The embryonic cells further differentiate into 3 layers. Innermost is the endoderm, which will develop into respiratory and digestive systems and some other internal body parts. The middle layer is the mesoderm, which will develop into bones, muscles, and the reproductive and excretory systems. The outermost layer, the ectoderm, will develop into the nervous system and sensory receptors—eyes, ears, nose, and skin. The amniotic sac, umbilical cord, and placenta develop along with the embryo.

Human development in utero follows 3 basic principles. One is cephalocaudal, or literally, from head to tail; that is, physical structures closer to the head develop earlier than those closer to the toes. Another principle is from more basic to more specialized. In other words, body organs and systems do not first appear as completely formed miniatures but in simpler earlier forms that only later develop finer details. For example, the heart first forms with 2chambers and later develops into an organ with 4 chambers. A third principle of human prenatal development is in the order of importance. The organs most important to survival, such as the brain and the heart, develop earliest, while other organs not as important for surviving develop later.

Fetal period

The fetal period follows the germinal and embryonic periods. It begins 2 months after conception and continues for an average of 7 months. At 3 months following conception, a fetus is almost 4 inches (about 10 cm) long and weighs a bit more than 2 ounces (60 grams). The fetus becomes physically active during this period, moving its limbs and head and opening and closing its mouth. The fetal forehead, face, eyelids, nose, chin, and hands are discernible. The lower fetal body parts undergo a growth spurt at around 4 months. Toenails and fingernails develop by 5 months; fetal activity increases. By the end of 6 months, fetal eyelids and eyes are completely formed; the fetus has developed the grasping reflex and begins to breathe intermittently. During the eighth and ninth months, the fetus develops fatty tissues; the functioning of the heart, kidneys, and other organs increases; and sensory systems begin working, especially hearing. Some children report memories of sounds like the maternal heartbeat; some remember music they heard in utero.

Prenatal brain development

The human brain begins forming 18 days after conception. It is among the slowest-developing organs and continues development after birth for many years. In a 9-weeks fetus, the brain makes up 25% of body weight, which decreases as the rest of the body develops. The brain is 10% of a newborn's body weight and 2% of an adult's. In the embryonic period, by the third week, the embryonic disc, which will become the baby, has formed the 3 germ layers of ectoderm, mesoderm, and endoderm. Cells in the ectoderm thicken, forming the neural plate, and a groove forms in this plate at around 18 days. This groove begins to close, creating the neural tube, which normally closes fully by 4 weeks. Failed or incomplete closure results in neural tube birth defects like anencephaly or spina bifida. Neural tube walls thicken to form the neuroepithelium, where glia, neurons, and all brain cells will develop.

Structures that develop prenatally in the brain following closure of the neural tube

After the neural tube closes at around 4 weeks in gestation, the forebrain, midbrain, and hindbrain differentiate. During this fourth week, the forebrain additionally divides into the diencephalon and telencephalon. Near the fourth week's end, the hindbrain divides into the metencephalon and myelencephalon. The forebrain's telencephalon grows to cover its diencephalon, forming the cerebral hemispheres and cortices by 11 weeks. The brain stem and the hindbrain develop earliest; then the midbrain and, finally, the forebrain's cerebral cortices develop. This sequence is believed by scientists to be connected to basic biological processes, like breathing and digestion, which must function immediately at birth, before the gray matter of the cerebral cortices, needed for thinking and other mental processes, will develop in the forebrain.

Cellular prenatal and postnatal brain development

Research has found that all of the neurons (brain cells) a human will ever have are produced by the end of the second trimester of gestation. As many as 250,000 cells per minute are formed between the 10th and 26th weeks after conception. Cellular overproduction is normal during prenatal development. Also normal is natural cellular death, known as *apoptosis* or *pruning,* which takes place before and after birth; an estimated 50% to70% of this pruning occurs postnatally. Once formed, neurons establish connections. Those not making connections or making improper ones die, that is, they are pruned, as part of the developmental process. Ultimately, the adult human brain contains approximately 100 billion neurons.

Cellular development in the brain before and after birth

The first stage of neuronal development, which occurs prenatally and is complete by the end of the second trimester of gestation, is proliferation, that is, the production of nerve cells. The second stage is cellular migration, occurring between the fourth and ninth months of gestation. Cells are first formed in the wall of the neural tube and then migrate to their ultimate destinations. Alongside of the developing neurons, radial glial cells grow to guide the formation of neural pathways for neurons to migrate to their final locations. The third stage of neuronal development continues beyond birth and involves 2 processes: myelinization and synaptogenesis. Myelinization is the process whereby myelin, a sheath of fatty tissue, develops around the neurons to insulate them from other cells, protect them, and facilitate the transmission of neural impulses along the nerves. Synaptogenesis is the process whereby neurons establish synapses—connections to communicate with each other and with end organs, enabling transmission of neural impulses throughout the brain and between the brain and other organs.

Fetal behaviors and their corresponding gestational ages in weeks

The first fetal movements are observed by 7 weeks of gestation. Startling and general motions occur at 8 weeks. Hiccups, isolated arm and leg movements, and isolated backward head bending occur at 9 weeks; isolated head rotation happens at 9 to 10 weeks. Isolated downward head bending, breathing movements, arm and leg twitches, stretching, rotation, and hand-face touching emerge at 10 weeks. Jaw movements appear at around 10 to 11 weeks, and fetuses have been observed to yawn at 11 weeks. Movements of the fingers, and sucking and swallowing movements, typically develop by 12 weeks of fetal development. Clonic movements, meaning short, spasmodic motions, of the fetal arms and legs are observed to occur by 13 weeks. The developing fetus will demonstrate motions associated with the rooting reflex (physically searching for the nipple to nurse) at 14 weeks of gestation. The fetus is found to make its first eye movements by the gestational age of 16 weeks.

Fetus behavioral states

Human fetuses are generally active throughout gestation. However, as they develop, their movements more clearly differentiate into active and inactive periods. Behavioral states, that is, well-defined, distinguishable sets of factors with stability across time and discrete transitions between them, have been observed by 36 weeks of gestation and identified based on newborn behavioral states as referents. Some describe these states as evidence of increased central nervous system integration. *Quiet sleep* (1F) involves a stable heart rate, no eye movements, and occasional startling. This occurs at c. 15% at 36 weeks; 32% at 38 weeks; and 38% at term. *Active sleep* (2F) includes eye movements, gross body movements, and heart rate often accelerating with movements. This occurs c. 42% to 48% of the time. *Quiet awake* (3F) involves eye movements; no body movements, no heart rate accelerations, and wider oscillation bandwidth than quiet sleep (1F) occur briefly and rarely. *Active awake* (4F) involves eye movements, constant activity, and an unstable and faster heart rate, occurring c. 6% to 7% of the time at 36 to 38 weeks and 9% c. 40 weeks, just before birth.

Hearing in the developing fetus

By 22 to 24 weeks of gestation, the fetus shows responses to sound by changes in movement. Frequency and pitch, intensity and loudness, and duration of sounds affect fetal responses. Louder sounds cause greater movement. Fetal hearing begins developing at 250 to 500 Hz, the lower range of frequencies humans can hear. This increases with development toward the adult hearing range of 20 to 20,000 Hz. Researchers have found fetuses also respond discriminatively to speech sounds, like different vowels. Fetuses can hear their mothers' heartbeats, blood flow, and digestive sounds. They can also hear sounds outside the womb, though these are attenuated (damped) by maternal tissues. Higher-frequency or pitched sounds above 2,000 Hz are attenuated by up to 40 dB (decibels), so the fetus likely cannot hear these. It is interesting to note that the basic frequency range of human speech, 125 to 250 Hz, is attenuated the least of all frequencies, enabling unborn babies to hear speech sounds coming from both the mother and from others around her.

Development of sense and smell in the fetus

From roughly 12 weeks of gestation, the human fetus begins swallowing amniotic fluid. This means that anything the mother ingests, which diffuses into the amniotic fluid, can be received by the fetus. Also, any changes in the maternal diet or other substances ingested change the kind of stimulation the fetus experiences. Because the sensory receptors for smell and taste in the fetal brain are both bathed in amniotic fluid, these 2 senses are difficult for scientists to separate. Hence, fetal responses to olfaction, or smell, and gustation, or taste, are typically combined under the term *chemosensation*. Researchers have found that, when they inject sugar into the amniotic fluid, fetuses swallow more; when a harmful substance, like iodinated poppy seed, is injected into the amniotic fluid, they swallow less. The facts that newborn infants orient toward their own amniotic fluid and prefer the odors of their mothers over those of other women are interpreted by scientists as additional evidence that babies experience smells and tastes before birth.

Experience of touch, temperature, and pain

Touch is the earliest fetal sense to develop at around 8 weeks' gestation. Fetuses around 8 to 9 weeks move their heads away from touch stimuli to the cheeks or lips; however, they move toward touch stimuli in the second trimester. Excepting the back and top of the head, most of the fetal body responds to touch by 14 weeks. Fetuses touch their faces with arms or hands from around 13 weeks, supplying tactile stimulation; twins, triplets, or other multiple pregnancies afford greater touch stimulation. Pregnant mothers report more fetal movement when they take hot baths; otherwise, the temperature regulation of normal pregnancy prevents fetuses from feeling much temperature variation. Neural pathways for pain develop around 26 weeks. Pain is subjective and can only be measured indirectly in fetuses, so whether they feel pain is controversial. However, behavioral reactions have been observed in fetuses when touched by a needle during amniocentesis, and after fetal scalp blood sampling during labor, and biochemical stress responses have been measured after needle punctures during blood transfusions from 23 weeks' gestation.

Reflexes in newborn infants

Reflexes are involuntary motor movements that are elicited by sensory or kinetic stimulation, for example, visual stimuli like light, tactile stimulation (touch), or changes in body position. Brain structures below the cerebral cortices control these reflexive motor behaviors. Many reflexes appear in newborns and disappear when they are several months old, for example, the Babinski reflex (when the sole of the foot is stroked, the toes fan out and then curl up), the Moro reflex (startling, extending the head and limbs at loud noises or sudden slipping), and rooting (searching for the nipple) and sucking reflexes. Rooting and sucking disappear as they are replaced by nonreflexive or voluntary eating behaviors. Reflexes like breathing and swallowing are necessary to survive and persist throughout life, as do blinking and yawning reflexes. Infant reflexes are important for indicating normal brain functioning and integrity, ensuring newborns' survival, and providing foundations for future motor development. Infant reflexes that are weaker than normal, or persist past ages when they normally end can indicate cerebral palsy or other neurological problems.

From birth to 4 or 5 months, infants demonstrate the rooting reflex when their cheeks or mouth edges are touched. From birth to 4 to 6 months, the sucking reflex is activated by touching their mouths. From birth to 4 months, babies show the grasping reflex when their hands are touched. The Moro, or startling, reflex results from sudden loud sounds, such as objects being dropped, and occurs from birth to 4 to 6 months. The Babinski reflex, wherein the baby's toes fan out and then curl up when the sole of the foot is stroked, appears from birth to 9 to 12 months. Babies demonstrate the swimming reflex, holding their breath and making swimming motions with their limbs when placed in water, from birth to 4 to 6 months. When infants are held above a surface and their feet touch it, they show the stepping reflex from birth to 3 to 4 months. From birth to 4 months, babies exhibit the labyrinthine reflex, extending limbs when placed on their backs and flexing limbs when placed on their stomachs. These reflexes normally disappear by the ends of the time ranges given.

Prenatal visual development

Of all senses, vision is the least stimulated and used in utero as there is no light source inside the womb and the fetus sees little more than a "diffuse orange glow," which may become lighter if very bright light is shined on the mother's abdomen or transvaginally at the cervix. Thus, infant vision is less developed than other senses upon birth, when infants receive all the same visual stimuli that adults do. The pupillary reflex, which expands and contracts the pupils to admit more or less light, is underdeveloped at birth. Visual accommodation for focusing on nearer or farther objects is also restricted at birth. It is clearest at around 7 to 20 inches, corresponding to the distance of the baby's eyes from the mother's face when nursing. The combination of poor pupillary reflexes and visual accommodation in neonates makes much of their vision unfocused. However, these abilities develop quickly after birth. As the baby grows, processes of tracking, scanning, and other eye movements additionally develop, enhancing eyesight.

Normative versus dynamic child physical development

Normative development refers to normal or typical abilities and limits of the majority of children in the same age and cultural groups. Developmental norms help parents know what their children should be able or unable to do at certain ages and what to expect. Developmental milestones identify certain physical abilities, behaviors demonstrating them, and ages when they typically emerge. For example, knowing the fine motor development of 3-year-olds is typically not ready to operate zippers informs parents that expecting this ability would be unrealistic. Dynamic development refers to physical changes occurring during children's development as they grow older and gain experience, the order of changes, and their interactions. Children's bodies grow in 3 directional patterns: (1) from large muscle to small muscle, or gross motor to fine motor—large trunk, neck, and limb muscles develop before small wrist, hand, finger, and eye muscles; children walk before self-feeding, scribbling, and so on; (2) top-to-bottom, or head to toe—infants can hold up their heads before they can crawl or walk; (3) proximodistal, or inner to outer. Central muscles nearer the trunk develop before extremity (hands, feet) muscles.

Physical growth of children

1. General to specific: Movements become more defined with development. Infants wave their limbs; older children can walk and draw.
2. Differentiation and integration: Differentiation is locating or isolating specific body parts and gaining control over them. Once differentiated, children integrate the movements of each part with those of others, enabling more complex motor activities like walking, riding bicycles, and so on.
3. Growth variations: Various body parts grow at different rates; children's motor abilities vary by age.
4. Optimal tendencies: Growth tends to seek optimal realization of its potential. If development is delayed, for example, by malnutrition, it tends to catch up when possible; hence children with such environmental delays can develop skills at later ages.
5. Sequential growth: Development proceeds in an ordered sequence, seen in the growth of individual body parts and motor behaviors—rolling over, then sitting up, then crawling, then walking.
6. Critical periods: Just as the first few years are critical for brain development, ages 1½ to 5 years are critical for motor development.

Motor development in children

Motor development means children's physical growth and growth in their abilities to use their bodies and bodily skills. The process whereby children gain skills and patterns in physical movement is also a common definition of motor development. Variables influencing motor development include genetic factors; the child's birth size, body composition, and body build; nutritional elements; birth order of the child; aspects of child rearing; the family's social class and socioeconomic status; the child's temperament type; the child's and family's ethnic group; and family cultural influences. Gross motor development involves use of the large muscles for sitting, standing, walking, running, jumping, reaching, throwing, and so on. Fine motor development involves the use of small muscles for self-feeding by hand and with utensils; picking up small objects, drawing, writing, tying shoes, brushing teeth, and so on.

Physical movement that children engage in

One type of physical movement is (1) locomotor movement, that is, the child's movement of his or her body from one location to another. Locomotor movement includes crawling, walking, running, jumping, hopping, skipping, galloping, and leaping. Locomotor movement helps to develop the child's gross motor skills. (2) Non-locomotor movement refers to the child's body movements made while remaining in the same location. Sitting down, standing up, wriggling, turning around, twisting, pulling, and pushing are activities that demonstrate non-locomotor movement, which helps to develop the child's skills of coordination and balance. (3) Manipulative movement is the child's controlled usage of the hands and feet, with and without objects. Activities like opening and closing the hands, grasping, waving, throwing, and catching are examples of manipulative movement, which helps to develop a child's hand-eye coordination and fine motor skills.

Erik Erikson's psychosocial theory of development

First Stage
Erikson proposed 8 stages of psychosocial development or *ages of man* through adulthood. He later added a ninth stage to include very old age. Each of Erikson's stages focuses on a *nuclear conflict* that the individual must resolve. According to Erikson's theory, from birth through 1½ to 2 years, children are in the stage of Basic Trust Versus Mistrust. In this first stage, if an infant's needs, such as feeding, changing, bathing, pain relief, physical holding and cuddling, and overall nurturing, are met timely, to satisfaction, and consistently, the infant develops a sense of basic trust in the world, emerging with a sense of security and optimism toward life. If the infant's needs are not met, are only met after delays, are insufficiently satisfied, or are met inconsistently or unpredictably, the child emerges with emotional and social characteristics of mistrust in the world and basic insecurity. Erikson's positive outcome for this stage is Hope.

Second Stage
Of 9 developmental stages covering the entire human life span, Erikson identified his second stage as centering on resolving the nuclear conflict of Autonomy Versus Shame and Self-Doubt, transpiring between about 1½ to 2 years and 3½ to 4 years of age. Children are learning to control their bodies during this stage, as exemplified by toilet training. They extend this developing ability from controlling their bodily functions to exerting control over their environments. As they experience control, they begin to assert their independence. Parents are familiar with the temper tantrums, loud expressions of "No," and so on, associated with what is often called the *Terrible Twos*. Children successfully resolving this conflict feel proud and self-assured; those who overexert control or are punished feel ashamed and doubt their own abilities. Erikson found that the positive outcome for successfully completing this stage is Will.

Third Stage
Erikson's theory encompasses the whole life span of humans, from birth to death. He associated the third stage with the ages between 3½ and 5 to 6 years, a period which he termed the *play age*. Erikson named this stage for the nuclear conflict that the child must resolve, of Initiative Versus Guilt. Children increase their exploration of the environment in this stage. Their imaginations develop. They engage in active play, including fantasy, which expands their repertoire of skills. An important social development in this stage is learning to cooperate with others. Whereas many 2-year-olds cannot share, most 4-year-olds have learned how. Children learn to lead and to follow. Those not allowed to take the initiative or those punished for it feel guilty and fearful, remain overly dependent on adults, and are not included or marginalized by peer groups. Their play skills and imagination are limited. While Erikson's negative outcome for this stage is Guilt, he deemed its successful completion as Purpose.

Fourth Stage
Of 9 stages covering human life, Erikson identified his fourth stage with what he termed the *school age.* This stage begins around age 5 to 6 years, coinciding with when children begin formal education in Western and developed societies, and continuing until adolescence. Hence, only the beginning of this stage applies to children through age 6. Erikson called this stage and its nuclear conflict to resolve *Industry Versus Inferiority*. Children beginning school must learn to follow formal rules. Unstructured, free preschool play is replaced by structured play with complex rules, often requiring teamwork, as in sports. Children's

activities of making and getting along with friends are extended as their social circles expand. Homework and structured extracurricular activities require increasing self-discipline. Children who have previously learned trust, autonomy, and initiative in Erikson's 3 earlier stages are prepared to develop industry for accomplishing tasks; those who learned mistrust, shame or self-doubt, and guilt will likely experience defeat, developing a sense of inferiority. Erikson's positive outcome for this stage is Competence.

Emotional and social development of toddlers 1 to 2 years old

As babies become toddlers, they begin to develop self-awareness. They realize they are individuals, independent and separate from other people. Hence, they begin developing the ability to realize others may have their own feelings. Developing the capacity to imagine what others feel enables toddlers to begin developing empathy for others. While toddlers also become more interested in their peers, they are not as likely to play interactively as young children at later ages (e.g., 3 to 4 years) do. Instead, they are most likely to engage in parallel play, wherein they play next to another child rather than directly with him or her. For example, a toddler might approach an older toddler and watch him or her play. With encouragement to play *with* the older child, the younger toddler will start playing alongside of the older one, observing and sometimes imitating him or her.

Scaffolding

Toddlers allowed to explore their environments, play, and pursue their own interests learn better than those who are overly directed or controlled. The concept of scaffolding involves supplying only as much support as a child needs to accomplish a task or activity he or she cannot perform independently and gradually withdrawing this support as the child's skills develop and performance becomes more autonomous. The aim is to prevent excessive frustration while still allowing the child to attack and master new challenges. For example, if a younger toddler is trying to insert a square peg into a round hole, the adult can show him or her how to move the peg over each hole and then drop it into the hole that fits. An adult can give an older toddler time to figure out how to put on shoes or boots. If the child shows frustration, the adult can align the shoes or boots with the corresponding feet and suggest holding onto a chair while balancing on 1 leg to insert the other foot. Praising process and effort, not just product or outcome, promotes confidence.

Conflict resolution in toddlers and young children

Toddlers and young children have not yet developed much self-control and impulse control. This means they want immediate gratification and have difficulty deferring it; they also have difficulty not acting on their impulses. These characteristics make it difficult for young children to share things with others and to follow rules. The fact that toddlers are also learning control of their bodies and environments, and thus asserting their wills, further impinges on sharing, cooperating, and conforming to rules. Adults can model sharing for them. They can set kitchen timers to illustrate the duration waiting for a turn in group activities. Young toddlers are unable to resolve conflicts through discussing them; when they become frustrated with waiting, adults can distract or redirect their attention with other stimuli or activities. Adults can help toddlers learn and practice the art of sharing by initiating games involving playing together, passing or tossing balls around a circle of children, taking turns hitting a Nerf ball, and so on.

Emotional and social development in 3- to 4-year-old children

As toddlers grow older, they begin playing more interactively with peers. They also engage in pretend play. For example, children might use toys like blocks to simulate food, "serve" playmates, pretend to exchange money, operate a toy cash register, and so on. They may act out killing monsters using toy weapons or dress up in parents' clothing and imitate adult behaviors like going to work. Most 3- to 4-year-olds are developing better abilities to share and take turns with peers than 1- to 2-year-olds, but they are still learning. Adults can encourage early friendships by providing some activities without sharing, such as individual artwork, playing musical instruments, and so on. When a child refuses to play with a peer, saying "Look at his (or her) face; how do you think he (or she) feels?" helps the child imagine how his or her actions affect others. Explaining others' feelings, for example, "Billy is sad because his daddy said good-bye," and suggesting pro-social comfort, for example, "Let's see if Billy wants to read a story with us," helps children see others' viewpoints, promoting empathy.

Optimal development of play activity

It is important to allow young children to choose the topics of play because this allows them to explore their own interests. For example, if a toddler is fascinated with trucks, adults can help him or her to construct pretend trucks, read books about trucks, and visit a local U-Haul to look at real trucks. When parents follow the child's lead by participating in children's pretend play, they teach him or her about playing interactively with others and its enjoyment and impart feelings of being important, competent, and loved in the child. They can also build upon child pretend play to promote learning. For example, if a child is pretending to have a picnic, the adult can ask the child, "What is good (or bad) weather for a picnic?" and "What kinds of foods are good (or bad) to pack for a picnic?"

Promoting emotional, social, and linguistic development

Toddlers often feel emotions quite clearly but have not yet developed the language skills to express them. This, combined with their limited abilities to control their behavior and refrain from acting on their impulses, is why they so frequently act out their feelings physically through tantrums, hitting others, and so on. Adults can help by putting emotions into words. For example, they can explain, "You are angry because your brother took your toy." They can also provide modeling by verbally articulating their own emotions: "I am frustrated because I can't find my keys." Helping them verbally label emotions and practice ways of managing them helps children eventually learn to practice these behaviors independently. Explaining consequences of children's actions, for example, "Stevie is crying because it hurt when you hit him—he feels sad and mad," helps them develop empathy and responsibility. Adults can ask or suggest what better choices the child can make next time to promote learning.

Using language development to promote sharing and cooperating, following rules, and observing limits and requests

By 3 years old, most children comprehend and utilize language well enough to understand simple verbal explanations. Adults can use children's linguistic development to promote their ongoing learning of social skills using simple language they can follow. For example, they can define limits and offer alternatives: "Hitting hurts; you may not hit. When you are mad, you can stomp your feet, jump up and down, rip up paper, throw soft toys, or ask me for a hug." Explaining natural consequences for their actions teaches cause-and-effect relationships: Throwing a hard toy has the consequence of putting the toy away; the positive consequence of cooperatively putting on coats is more time at the playground. Adults should explain the benefits of rules to children: Sharing toys gives everyone a chance to play; helping after-meal cleanup by taking their plates to the kitchen allows more time for stories. This enables children to understand reasons for limits and requests, teaches them to follow rules, and helps them eventually learn to make positive choices.

Language development

Conception to 6 months
Scientists have found evidence that fetuses can hear speech sounds made by their mothers and others around her while still in the womb. They learn to recognize their mother's voice before birth. Newborns listen to people speaking around them. They awaken at loud noises and startle or cry at unexpected noises. They quiet and attend to new sounds. From birth to 3 months, babies turn toward people speaking and smile at the sounds of their voices. They recognize familiar voices and stop crying upon hearing them. They also cease whatever activity they are involved in on hearing the sound of an unfamiliar voice, paying close attention. When someone speaks in comforting tones to babies up to 4 months old, they frequently respond to these whether they are familiar with the speaker's voice or not. By 3 months, they make sounds differentially expressing pleasure, hunger, pain, and so on. At around 4 to 6 months, babies respond to the word "no" and vocal tone changes, begin babbling, and communicate needs through sounds and gestures.

6 to 12 months of age
At 6 months, most babies vocalize expressively, especially babbling. They incorporate the same intonational patterns into babbling that they hear in adult speech, imitating adult rhythms, pitch changes, and so on. Receptively, they respond to hearing their names. Without visual input, they respond to others' voices by turning their heads or eyes toward the speakers. They show emotional understanding of voices by responding appropriately to friendly and angry tones. From 7 to 12 months, babies listen when spoken to, start enjoying games like peekaboo and patty-cake, and recognize names of familiar people or things like *mommy, daddy, car, phone, key,* and so on. They begin to respond to requests such as "Give the book to Mommy" and questions like "More milk?" By 12 months, babies understand simple directions, especially when accompanied by physical or vocal cues. They can use 1 or more words meaningfully. They realize the social import of speech. They practice using intonations and begin to utter their first words, for example, *Mama, doggie, night-night,* and *bye-bye.*

1 to 2 years old
Typically, 1-year-olds can point to pictures of things named by adults and point to some body parts on request. They can follow simple directions, for example, "Hot! Don't touch!" or "Pull the wagon" and understand simple questions, like "Where's the kitty?" or "What do you have in your bag?" They enjoy hearing adults recite rhymes and sing songs and listening to simple stories. They like having the same rhyme, game, or story repeated multiple times. By 18 months, most children have expressive vocabularies of around 5 to 20 words, mostly nouns. Their speech includes much "jargon," that is, nonword or unintelligible speech, which however, expresses emotional content through tone, volume, pitch, rhythm, and so on. They may display some echolalia, that is, repeating what others say or repeating the

same word or phrase over and over. Children from 18 months to 2 years old generally speak in utterances of 1 or 2 words at a time, though these utterances can express the same meaning as sentences, for example, "Heavy!" upon lifting something or "Watch this!" before doing something.

Generally, 2-year-olds can follow 2-step directions, for example, "Take your shirt off, and put it in the hamper." They now understand the concept of words indicating opposites, like hot and cold or stop and go. They can name more familiar objects in their environments. They can use at least 2 prepositions, commonly *in, on,* or *under.* They can utter short sentences; even 2-word utterances are now chiefly noun–verb combinations. Normally, at this age ⅔ of what a child says should be intelligible to adults. From ages 2 to 3 years, children's vocabularies expand greatly to around 150 to 300 words. The fluency and rhythm of their speech is normally still not well developed, and they do not yet control the loudness and pitch of their voices well. While they frequently confuse *I* and *me,* they can use *you* and *I* or *me* appropriately. They begin to use the possessives *mine* and *my.* They can follow requests such as "Show me your ears (or nose, eyes, mouth, or hair)."

3 and 4 years old
Typically, 3-year-olds comprehend who, what, or where questions and respond when called from another room. They should not be expected to answer all questions asked of them even when they understand. A child should be able to say his or her name, age, and sex when asked. They can now think through and answer questions like what they should do when hungry, thirsty, sleepy, or cold. They understand most simple questions about their surroundings and activities. They can recount their experiences understandably to adults. About 90% of 3-year-olds' speech should be intelligible to adults. They know the main body parts and can either name or point to them. Between 3 and 4 years, children develop expressive vocabularies of around 900 to 1,000 words. They can easily utter 3-word sentences. Verbs become more prevalent than earlier nouns. They correctly use the pronouns *I, me,* and *you* and begin using some past tenses and plurals. They commonly use the prepositions *in, on,* and *under* and may know more than 3 prepositions.

4 to 5 years of age
Most 4-year-olds understand almost everything they hear, speak more clearly, and can answer simple questions about stories they hear. They know familiar animals' names. They understand and can use at least 4 prepositions. They can name common objects in pictures and 1 or more colors. They usually can repeat 4-syllable words they hear and repeat 4 numerical digits if dictated slowly. They show comprehension of the concepts denoted by the prepositions *over* and *under* and of comparatives like *longer* or *shorter* and *bigger* or *smaller.* Between the ages of 4 and 5 years, children can easily follow directions even when the objects referenced in the directions are out of their sight. They do much practice, repeating speech sounds, syllables, phrases, and words. They tend to verbalize copiously during activities, narrating their actions. Psychologist Lev Vygotsky termed this *private speech.* They engage in much pretend play with narration. They can now correctly pronounce most vowels and the bilabial consonants /p/, /b/, /m/, /w/, and also /n/. They are likely still to distort other consonants somewhat.

5-year-old children
Commonly, 5-year-olds are able to count verbally to 10 and know numerical concepts of 4 or more. They understand and use most basic opposite concepts, for example, heavy versus light, hard versus soft, and big versus little. They can now speak with spontaneous use of

adjectives and adverbs to describe things. While some may have imperfect articulation, all of their speech should be intelligible to others. They should be able to pronounce all vowels and, in addition to consonants /p/, /b/, /m/, /w/, and /n/ mastered earlier, have added /h/, /k/, /g/, /t/, /d/, /ŋ / (ng), and /y/. They should also be able to repeat heard sentences up to 9 words long. They typically can follow uninterrupted 3-step directions. They know their age. They understand basic temporal concepts of day, night, morning, afternoon; today, yesterday, tomorrow; and while, after, and later. They should be able to define common terms like *chair, shoe,* or *hat* by their uses. They speak in longer sentences, including some complex and compound sentences. Overall, 5-year-old children's speech is grammatically correct.

6-year-old-children
Most children have mastered vowel sounds and the consonants /p/, /b/, /m/, /w/, /n/, /h/, /k/, /g/, /t/, /d/, /ŋ / (ng), and /y/ by around the age of 5 years. By the age of 6 years, they generally have also mastered the more difficult consonants /f/, /v/, /ʃ/ (sh), /ʒ/ (zh), and /đ/ (voiced *th* as in *the*). Most 6 year-olds should have numerical concepts up to 7. By age 6, children's speech normally is completely understandable to others and is also useful for social purposes. When a 6-year-old is shown a picture, he or she should be able to tell a contiguous story about it, including relationships among the elements. At 6 years old, children should also be able to verbalize relationships between things, people, and events in a connected fashion. Many 6-year-olds have not perfected pronunciation of the most difficult consonants /s/, /z/, /r/, /θ/ (devocalized *th* as in *earth*), /tʃ/ (ch), /dʒ/ (j), and /wh/, usually mastering these by age 7. Typically 6-year-olds are learning to read and write.

Monitoring and adjusting speech based on auditory feedback

When adults and older children are speaking, they tend to rely on their hearing to monitor their own speech for correct pronunciation. As a violinist plays, if a note produced is out of tune, the player will adjust his or her finger position, raising or lowering the pitch to correct it. Adult and older child speakers use an analogous process. Recent research (2011, 2012) has confirmed this: When participants wear headphones and hear altered vowel sounds while speaking, they adjust their spoken vowels accordingly. However, researchers have found that 2-year-olds do not use this process of responding to the auditory feedback of hearing their own voices to adjust their speech sounds. Scientists still do not know exactly what strategies toddlers might use in learning to control their speech. Some speculate that they may depend on the interaction with their listener(s), using visual, nonverbal, and verbal feedback from the other person(s) to assess the accuracy of the speech sounds they produce.

Perceptual development

6 to 9 months old
Perceptual development is important because it informs the motor activities of babies. They use their perception, for example, of slippery, slanted, rigid, or bumpy surfaces to gauge how to crawl or walk on them. Babies 6 to 9 months old will pick up, look at, and mouth objects to explore them. Hearing footsteps in a dark room, they may turn their heads to look for the source. They may display excitement when recognizing the color of a preferred food. Intersensory redundancy, that is, the overlapping of senses, provides multimodal perception, a foundation of perceptual development, as when an infant turns his or her head upon simultaneously seeing a face and hearing a voice. Perceptual development informs cognitive development. For example, perceiving differences and similarities enables the

cognitive ability of classification. Perceptual development is also important to the emotional and social development of young children. For example, they observe others' facial expressions and learn to interpret them as associated with particular emotional states and with social messages, such as encouragement, warning, or disapproval.

Up to around 18 months old

Children 9 to 17 months old stop crawling when they reach the edge of a surface. They will nuzzle fresh laundry to smell it; crumple and tear paper; touch, pat, push, squeeze, and otherwise explore textures; and manipulate substances like play dough. They remember the locations of objects they have seen before. They react to extreme temperatures and tastes. Between the ages of 12 and 18 months, toddlers learn to adjust their gaits according to the surfaces they are walking on, such as walking faster on smooth surfaces and slower on bumpy or rocky ones. Toddlers may decide to slide down a hill on their bottoms rather than walk after using perception to judge its steepness. When standing, toddlers often sway, bounce, or swing their arms to music. They pull their hands away from slimy or unfamiliar textures they touch. When playing at the beach or in a sandbox, they often spend a long time burying their hands or feet in the sand. They will stop pouring sand into a pail when they see it is full.

18 to 36 months

From 18 to 24 months, toddlers are likely to engage in and enjoy rough-and-tumble play. Around 2 years of age, they learn to handle fragile objects gently. Most 2-year-olds enjoy books with tactile stimuli, like fuzzy, fake fur; soft, plush fabric; and sandpaper. At 2 to 3 years, many children enjoy playing with sand and water by digging, filling pails, and pouring. By age 3, children can identify blankets and other familiar objects by touch alone. They can identify distinctive toy shapes buried in sand by feeling them. They learn to climb more slowly near the tops of ladders. They know to press harder on clay than play dough and to walk more slowly and carefully when carrying an uncovered container of liquid than when carrying one with a lid. Most 3-year-olds have developed the ability to use their eyesight to follow the lines that they mark on paper when scribbling. They can also observe an adult or older child draw a circle and then try to imitate it.

Responding directly to environments to representing them symbolically

Just as children's cognitive development generally proceeds from more concrete to more abstract, this progression can be seen in their responses to the environment moving from the sensorimotor or behavioral to the symbolic or representational. For example, very young children can navigate their homes by recalling visual images of objects, their locations, and other sensory information; as they grow older, they learn abstract concepts like left and right or how to read a floor plan of their home. Researchers find that young children aged around 2 years start reconstructing and symbolically representing what they know. Toddlers often use available objects to symbolize other objects during pretend play. For example, a child might pretend a broom is a horse to ride or a guitar to strum, or a calculator is a smartphone, and so on. Their capacity to employ different media and modalities expands: By preschool ages, they may incorporate gestures, body, and spoken language; drawing, painting, or sculpture; construction; dramatic enactions; and written language. These multimodal play representations of concepts reciprocally improve children's actual knowledge.

Causes of intellectual disabilities in babies and young children

Infections
Congenital cytomegalovirus (CMV) is passed to fetuses from mothers, who may be asymptomatic. About 90% of newborns are also asymptomatic; 5% to 10% of these have later problems. Of the 10% born with symptoms, 90% will have later neurological abnormalities, including intellectual disabilities. Congenital rubella, or German measles, is also passed to fetuses from unvaccinated and exposed mothers, causing neurological damage including blindness or other eye disorders, deafness, heart defects, and intellectual disabilities. Congenital toxoplasmosis is passed to fetuses by infected mothers, who can be asymptomatic, with a parasite from raw or undercooked meat that causes intellectual disabilities, vision or hearing loss, and other conditions. Encephalitis is brain inflammation caused by infection, most often viral. Meningitis is inflammation of the meninges, or membranes, covering the brain and is caused by viral or bacterial infection; the bacterial form is more serious. Both encephalitis and meningitis can cause intellectual disabilities. Maternal human immunodeficiency virus (HIV) and acquired immunodeficiency syndrome (AIDS) can be passed to fetuses, destroying immunity to infections, which can cause intellectual disabilities. Maternal listeriosis, a bacterial infection from contaminated food, animals, soil, or water, can cause meningitis and intellectual disabilities in surviving fetuses and infants.

Chromosomal abnormalities
A missing part of chromosome 5 causes cri du chat syndrome, named for the infant's characteristic high-pitched, catlike cry; it causes intellectual disabilities, among other abnormalities. In addition to such chromosomal deletions, there are chromosomal translocations, wherein genes are either positioned in different locations on the chromosome or located on different chromosomes than normally; these can also cause intellectual disabilities. Chromosomal defects causing intellectual disabilities include fragile X syndrome, a mutation in the FMR1 gene that makes a small part of the gene code repeat on a fragile portion of the X chromosome, causing the commonest form of inherited intellectual disabilities in boys. Another chromosomal defect occurs in Prader-Willi syndrome, caused by a missing gene on a part of chromosome 15. Along with other symptoms, Prader-Willi causes small size, floppiness, intellectual disabilities, reduced or absent sex hormones, and an uncontrollable urge to eat everything. Another chromosomal abnormality involves errors in the numbers of chromosomes, as in Down syndrome, caused by an extra third copy of chromosome 21, which produces varying degrees of intellectual disabilities.

Environmental, nutritional, and metabolic influences
Environmental deprivation syndrome results when developing children are deprived of necessary environmental elements—physical, including adequate nourishment (malnutrition); climate or temperature control (extremes of heat or cold); hygiene, like changing and bathing; and so on. It also includes lack of adequate cognitive stimulation, which can stunt a child's intellectual development, and neglect in general. Malnutrition results from starvation; vitamin, mineral, or nutrient deficiency; deficiencies in digesting or absorbing foods; and some other medical conditions. Environmental radiation, depending on dosage and time of exposure, can cause intellectual disabilities. Congenital hypothyroidism (underactive thyroid) can cause intellectual disabilities, as can hypoglycemia (low blood sugar) from inadequately controlled diabetes or occurring independently and infant hyperbilirubinemia. Bilirubin, a waste product of old red blood

cells, is found in bile made by the liver and is normally removed by the liver; excessive bilirubin buildup in babies can cause intellectual disabilities. Reye syndrome, caused by aspirin given children with flu or chicken pox, or following these viruses or other upper respiratory infections, or from unknown causes, produces sudden liver and brain damage and can result in intellectual disabilities.

Genetic or inherited metabolic disorders

Adrenoleukodystrophy is an X-linked genetic trait. Some female carriers have mild forms, but it affects more males more seriously. It impairs metabolism of very long-chain fatty acids, which build up in the nervous system (as well as adrenal glands and male testes). The childhood cerebral form, manifesting at ages 4 to 8, causes seizures, visual and hearing impairments, receptive aphasia, dysgraphia, dysphagia, intellectual disabilities, and other effects. Galactosemia is an inability to process galactose, a simple sugar in lactose, or milk sugar. By-product buildup damages the liver, kidneys, eyes, and brain. Hunter syndrome, Hurler syndrome, and Sanfilippo syndrome each cause the lack of different enzymes; all cause an inability to process mucopolysaccharides or glycosaminoglycans (long sugar-molecule chains). Hurler and Sanfilippo (but not Hunter) syndromes are autosomal recessive traits, meaning both parents must pass on the defect. All cause progressive intellectual disabilities. Lesch-Nyhan syndrome, affecting males, is a metabolic deficiency in processing purines. It causes hemiplegia, varying degrees of intellectual disabilities, and self-injurious behaviors. Phenylketonuria (PKU), an autosomal recessive trait, causes lack of the enzyme to process dietary phenylalanine, resulting in intellectual disabilities.

Genetic abnormalities and syndromes affecting the nervous system

Rett syndrome is a nervous system disorder causing developmental regression, particularly severe in expressive language and hand function. It is associated with a defective protein gene on an X chromosome. Having 2 X chromosomes, females with the defect on 1 of them can survive; with only 1 X chromosome, males are either miscarried, stillborn, or die early in infancy. Rett syndrome produces many symptoms, including intellectual disabilities. Tay-Sachs disease, an autosomal recessive disorder, is a nervous system disease caused by a defective gene on chromosome 15 resulting in a missing protein for breaking down gangliosides, chemicals in nerve tissues that build up in cells, particularly brain neurons, causing damage. Tay-Sachs is more prevalent in Ashkenazi Jews. The adult form is rare; the infantile form is commonest, with nerve damage starting in utero. Many symptoms, including intellectual disabilities, appear at 3 to 6 months and death occurs by 4 to 5 years. Tuberous sclerosis, caused by genetic mutations, produces tumors damaging the kidneys, heart, skin, brain, and central nervous system. Symptoms include intellectual disabiltiies, seizures, and developmental delays.

Prescription drugs, substances of abuse, social drugs, and diseases in pregnant mothers

Warfarin, a prescription anticoagulant drug to thin the blood and prevent excessive clotting, can cause microcephaly (undersized head) and intellectual disabilities in an infant when the mother has taken it during pregnancy. The prescription antiseizure drug Trimethadione can cause developmental delays in babies when it has been taken by pregnant mothers. Maternal abuse of solvent chemicals during pregnancy can also cause microcephaly and intellectual disabilities. Maternal crack cocaine abuse during pregnancy can cause severe and profound intellectual disabilities and many other developmental defects in fetuses, which become evident when they are newborns. Maternal alcohol abuse can cause fetal alcohol syndrome, which often includes intellectual disabilities, among many other symptoms. Maternal rubella (German measles) virus can cause intellectual disabilities as well as visual and hearing impairments and heart defects. Maternal herpes simplex virus can cause microcephaly, intellectual disabilities, and microophthalmia (small or no eyes). The varicella (chicken pox) virus in pregnant mothers can also cause intellectual disabilities as well as muscle atrophy in babies.

General characteristics of infants and young children with intellectual disabilities

Newborns with intellectual disabilities, especially of greater severity, may not demonstrate normal reflexes, such as rooting and sucking reflexes, necessary for nursing. They may not show other temporary infant reflexes such as the Moro, Babinski, swimming, stepping, or labyrinthine reflexes, or they may demonstrate weaker versions of some of these. In some babies, these reflexes will exist but persist past the age when they normally disappear. Babies with intellectual disabilities are likely to display developmental milestones at later-than-typical ages. The ages when they do display milestones vary according to the severity of the disability and by individual. Young children with intellectual disabilities are likely to walk, self-feed, and speak later than normally developing children. Those who learn to read and write do so at later ages. Children with mild intellectual disabilities may lack curiosity and have quiet demeanors; those with profound intellectual disabilities are likely to remain infantile in abilities and behaviors throughout life. Intellectually disabled children will score below normal on standardized IQ tests and adaptive behavior rating scales.

Variables having the potential to cause learning disabilities (LDs) in young children

LDs are basically neurological disorders. Though they are more specific to particular areas of learning than global disorders like intellectual disabilities, scientific research has found correlations between LDs and many of the same factors that cause intellectual disabilities, including prenatal influences like excessive alcohol or other drug consumption, diseases, and so on. Once babies are born, glandular disorders, brain injuries, exposure to secondhand smoke or other toxins, infections of the central nervous system, physical trauma, or malnutrition can cause neurological damage resulting in LDs. Hypoxia and anoxia (oxygen loss) before, during, or after birth is a cause, as are radiation and chemotherapy. These same influences often cause behavioral disorders as well as LDs. Another factor is genetic: Both LDs and behavior disorders have been observed to run in families. While research has not yet identified specific genetic factors, heritability does appear to be a component in influencing learning and behavioral disorders.

Neurological damage that has been found in children with learning disabilities (LDs) and attention deficit hyperactivity (ADHD) disorder

Various neurological research studies have revealed that children diagnosed with LDs and ADHD have at least 1 of several kinds of structural damage to their brains. Scientists have found smaller numbers of cells in certain important regions of the brains of some children with learning and behavioral disorders. Some of these children are found to have brain cells of smaller than normal size. In some cases, dysplasia is discovered; that is, some brain cells migrate into the wrong area of the brain. In some children with learning and behavioral disorders, blood flow is found to be lower than normal to certain regions in the brain. Also, the brain cells of some children with learning and behavioral disabilities show lower levels of glucose metabolism; glucose (blood sugar) is the brain's main source of fuel, so inadequate utilization of glucose can affect the brain's ability to perform some functions related to cognitive processing, as in LDs, and to attention and impulse control, as in ADHD.

Types of learning disabilities (LDs)

Dyslexia, the most common LD, means deficiency or inability in reading. It primarily affects reading but can also interfere with writing and speaking. Characteristics include reversing letters and words, for example, confusing *b* and *d* in reading and writing; reading *won* as *now*, confusing similar speech sounds like /p/ and /b/, and perceiving spaces between words in the wrong places when reading. Dyscalculia is difficulty doing mathematical calculations; it can also affect using money and telling time. Dysgraphia means difficulties specifically with writing, including omitting words in writing sentences or leaving sentences unfinished, difficulty putting one's thoughts into writing, and poor handwriting. Central auditory processing disorder causes difficulty perceiving small differences in words despite normal hearing acuity; for example, *couch and chair* may be perceived as *cow and hair*. Background noise and information overloads exacerbate the effects. Visual processing disorders affect visual perception despite normal visual acuity, causing difficulty finding information in printed text or from maps, charts, pictures, graphs, and so on; synthesizing information from various sources into 1 place; and remembering directions to locations.

Attachment styles identified in toddlers by Mary Ainsworth

Mary Ainsworth worked with John Bowlby, discovering the first empirical evidence supporting his attachment theory. From her *Strange Situation* experiments, she identified secure, insecure and avoidant, insecure and resistant, and insecure and disorganized attachment styles. Securely attached children show normal separation anxiety when mother leaves and happiness when she returns, avoid strangers when alone but are friendly with mother present, and use mother as a safe base for environmental exploring. Insecure and resistant children show exaggerated separation anxiety, ambivalence and resistance to mother upon reuniting, fear strangers, cry more, and explore less than secure or avoidant babies. Insecure and avoidant children show no separation anxiety or stranger anxiety and little interest on reunions with mother and are comforted equally by mother or strangers. Insecure and disorganized types seem dazed and confused, respond inconsistently, and may mix resistant and ambivalent and avoidant behaviors. Secure styles are associated with sensitive, responsive caregiving and children's positive self-images and other images, resistant and ambivalent styles with inconsistent caregiving, and avoidant with unresponsive caregivers. Avoidant, resistant, and disorganized styles, associated with negative self-images and low self-esteem, are most predictive of emotional disturbances.

Emotional disturbances in young children

Researchers have investigated emotional disturbances but have not yet established known causes for any. Some disturbances, for example the major mental illness schizophrenia, seem to run in families and hence include a genetic component; childhood schizophrenia exists as a specific diagnosis. Factors contributing to emotional disturbances can be biological or environmental but more often are likely a combination of both. Dysfunctional family dynamics can often contribute to child emotional disorders. Physical and psychological stressors on children can also contribute to the development of emotional problems. Some people have attributed emotional disturbances to diet, and scientists have also researched this but have not discovered proof of cause and effect. Bipolar disorder is often successfully treated with the chemical lithium, which affects sodium flow through nerve cells, so chemical imbalance may be implicated as an etiology. Pediatric bipolar disorder, which has different symptoms than adult bipolar disorder, correlates highly with histories of bipolar and other mood disorders or alcoholism in both parents.

Anxiety disorders

Anxiety disorders include generalized anxiety disorder (GAD), obsessive-compulsive disorder (OCD), posttraumatic stress disorder (PTSD), panic disorder, social phobia, and specific phobias. All share a common characteristic of overwhelming, irrational, and unrealistic fears. GAD involves excessive worrying about anything or everything and free-floating anxiety. Anxiety may be about real issues but is nonetheless exaggerated and spreads, overtaking the child's life. OCD involves obsessive and preoccupied thoughts and compulsive or irresistible actions, including often bizarre rituals. Germ phobia, constant hand washing, repeatedly checking whether tasks are done or undone, and collecting things excessively are common. PTSD follows traumatic experiences/events. Children have frequent, extreme nightmares, crying, flashbacks wherein they vividly perceive or believe they are experiencing the traumatic event again, insomnia, depression, anxiety, and social withdrawal. Symptoms of panic disorder are panic attacks involving extreme fear and physical symptoms like a racing heart, cold hands and feet, pallor, hyperventilation, and feeling unable to move. Children with social phobia develop fear and avoidance of day care, preschool, or other social settings. Specific phobias are associated with specific objects, animals, or persons and are often triggered by traumatic experiences involving these.

Pediatric bipolar disorder

Bipolar, formerly called manic-depressive disorder, has similar depressive symptoms in children as adults. However, children's mood swings often occur much faster, and children show more symptoms of anger and irritability than other adult manic symptoms. Bipolar children's most common symptoms include frequent mood swings; extreme irritability; protracted (up to several hours) tantrums or rages; separation anxiety; oppositional behavior; hyperactivity, impulsivity, and distractibility; restlessness and fidgetiness; silly, giddy, or goofy behavior; aggression; racing thoughts; grandiose beliefs or behaviors; risk-taking; depressed moods; lethargy; low self-esteem; social anxiety; hypersensitivity to environmental or emotional triggers; carbohydrate (sugar or starch) cravings; and trouble getting up in the morning. Other common symptoms include bed-wetting (especially in boys), night terrors, pressured or fast speech, obsessive or compulsive behaviors, motor and vocal tics, excessive daydreaming, poor short-term memory, poor organization, learning disabilities, morbid fascinations, hypersexuality, bossiness and manipulative behavior, lying, property destruction, paranoia, hallucinations, delusions, and suicidal ideations. Less common symptoms include migraines, bingeing, self-injurious behaviors, and animal cruelty.

Conduct disorder

Factors contributing to conduct disorders in children include genetic predispositions, neurological damage, child abuse, and other traumatic experiences. Children with conduct disorders display characteristic emotional and behavioral patterns. These include aggression: They bully or intimidate others, often start physical fights, will use dangerous objects as weapons, exhibit physical cruelty to animals or humans, and assault and steal from others. Deliberate property destruction is another characteristic—breaking things or setting fires. Young children are limited in some of these activities by their smaller size, lesser strength, and lack of access; however, they show the same types of behaviors against smaller, younger, weaker, or more vulnerable children and animals, along with oppositional and defiant behaviors against adults. Also, while truancy is impossible or unlikely in

- 45 -

preschoolers, and running away from home is less likely, young children with conduct disorders are likely to demonstrate some forms of seriously violating rules, another symptom of this disorder.

Psychotic disorders

Psychosis is a general psychiatric category referring to thought disturbances or disorders. The most common symptoms are delusions that is, believing things that are not true, and hallucinations, that is, seeing, hearing, feeling, tasting, or smelling things that are not there. While early childhood psychosis is rarer than at later ages, psychiatrists confirm it does occur. Moreover, prognosis is poorer for psychosis with onset in early childhood than in adolescence or adulthood. Causes can be from known metabolic or brain disorders or unknown. Younger children are more vulnerable to environmental stressors. Also, in young children, thoughts distorted by fantasy can be from normal cognitive immaturity, due to lack of experience and a larger range of normal functioning, or pathology; where they lie on this continuum must be determined by clinicians. Believing one is a superhero who can fly can be vivid imagination or delusional; having imaginary friends can be pretend play or hallucinatory. Other developmental disorders can also cloud differential diagnosis.

Childhood-onset schizophrenia

The incidence of childhood-onset schizophrenia is rare, but it does exist. One example of differential diagnosis involves distinguishing qualitatively between true auditory hallucinations and young children's "hearing voices" otherwise: In the latter case, a child hears his or her own or a familiar adult's voice in his or her head and does not seem upset by it, while in the former, a child may hear other voices, seemingly in his or her ears, and is frightened and confused by them. Tantrums, defiance, aggression, and other acting-out, externalized behaviors are less frequent in childhood-onset schizophrenia than internalized developmental differences, for example, isolation, shyness, awkwardness, fickleness, strange facial expressions, mistrust, paranoia, anxiety, and depression. Children demonstrate nonpsychotic symptoms earlier than psychotic ones. However, it is difficult to use prepsychotic symptoms as predictors due to variance among developmental peculiarities. While psychiatrists find the course of childhood-onset schizophrenia somewhat more variable than in adults, child symptoms resemble adult symptoms. Childhood-onset schizophrenia is typically chronic and severe, responds less to medication, and has a more guarded prognosis than adolescent- or adult-onset schizophrenia.

Visual impairments (VI) in babies and young children

Syndrome-related and other malformations like cleft iris or lens dislocation causing VI can have prenatal origins. Cataracts clouding the eye's lens can be congenital, traumatic, or due to maternal rubella. Eyes can be normal, but impairment in the brain's visual cortex can cause VI. Infantile glaucoma, like adult glaucoma, causes intraocular fluid buildup pressure and VI. Conjunctivitis and other infections cause VI. Strabismus and nystagmus are ocular-muscle conditions, respectively causing eye misalignments and involuntary eye movements. Trauma damaging the eyeball(s) is another VI cause. The optic nerve can suffer from atrophy (dysfunction) or hypoplasia, that is, developmental regression, usually prenatally due to neurological trauma; acuity cannot be corrected. Refractive errors like nearsightedness, farsightedness, and astigmatism are correctable. Retinoblastoma, or behind-the-eye tumors, can cause blindness and fatality; surgical or chemotherapeutic treatment is usually required before age 2. Premature infants can have retinopathy of prematurity or retrolental fibroplasia. Cryotherapeutic treatment seems to stop disease progression. Its effects range from none to severe VI (approximately 25% of children) to complete blindness.

Historically, it was thought that VI children developed more slowly than normal; however, it is now known that ages for reaching developmental milestones are equally variable in VI babies as in others and that they acquire milestones within equal age ranges. One developmental difference is in sequence: VI children tend to utter their first words or subject-verb 2-word sentences earlier than other children. Some VI children also demonstrate higher levels of language development at younger-than-typical ages. For example, they may sing songs from memory or recall events from the past at earlier ages than other children. This is a logical development in children who must rely more on input to their hearing and other senses than to their vision when the latter is impaired. Totally blind babies reach for objects later, hence explore the environment later; hand use, eye-hand coordination, and gross and fine motor skills are delayed. Blind infants' posture control develops normally (rolling, sitting, all-fours, and standing), but mobility (raising on arms, pulling up, and walking) are delayed.

Impacts of blindness

Cognitive development
Blind children have more difficulty determining and confirming characteristics of things, hence defining concepts and organizing them into more abstract levels; their problem-solving is active but harder, and they construct different realities than sighted children. Blind babies typically acquire object permanence (the understanding that unseen objects still exists) a year later than normal; they learn to reach for objects only by hearing. Understanding cause-and-effect relationships is difficult without visual evidence. Blind babies and toddlers take longer to understand and object's constancy regardless of their orientation in space, affecting their ability to orient toys and their own hands. Blind children can identify object size differences and similarities, but classifying object differences and similarities in other attributes requires longer times and more exposures to various similar objects. Blind children's development of the abilities to conserve object properties like material or substance, weight, amount and volume, length, and liquid volume is later than normal.

Emotional and social development
Blind babies and children are more dependent than others on adults, affecting development. With control of their inner realities but not of their outer environments, blind children may withdraw, seeking and responding less to social interaction. They may not readily develop concepts of the external world or self-concepts as beings separate from the world and the understanding that they can be both agents and recipients of actions relative to the environment. Mother-infant smiling initiates recognition, attachment, and communication in sighted babies; blind infants smile on hearing mother's voice at 2 months. Only tactile stimuli like tickling and nuzzling evoke regular smiling in blind babies. Missing facial expressions and other visual cues, blind children have more complicated social interactions. They often do not understand the basics of playing with others and seem emotionally ambivalent or uninterested and uncommunicative. Peers may reject or avoid them; adults often overprotect them. Self-help skills like chewing, scooping, self-feeding, teeth brushing, grooming, and toilet training are delayed in blind children.

Language development

Typically, children learn much by imitating others, which also initiates their understanding of symbolic meanings. Blind infants and children have the disadvantage of inability to observe others visually. They require systematic instruction, for example, using hearing and tactile methods like finger spelling, to develop imitation. They may babble and imitate language earlier than normal children but likely combine words to express needs later than normal. They use language mainly to meet immediate needs and describe current activities, using fewer adjectives and questions than other children. Blind children's early language reflects their knowledge of others' language more than their own developing knowledge of the environment. They may learn speech sounds but not their meanings; some are echolalic or otherwise repeat phrases or sentences out of context. They do not easily translate their sensory experiences into language. Delayed self-concept development can cause blind children to confuse personal pronouns (I and me, you, he or she, him or her, they, them, it). Fear of the unknown and overprotective adults can inhibit blind children's environmental exploration, delaying their concept and language development.

Prevalence and some etiologies of hearing impairment

Half or more (50% to 60%) of infant hearing losses have genetic origins—Down and other genetically based syndromes or the existence of parental hearing loss. About 25% or more of infant hearing losses are caused by maternal infections during pregnancy, such as cytomegalovirus (CMV), postnatal complications like blood transfusions or infection with meningitis, or traumatic head injuries. Included in this 25% or more are babies having nongenetic neurological disorders or conditions that affect their hearing. Malformations of the ears, head, or face can cause hearing loss in babies. Babies spending 5 days or longer in neonatal intensive care units (NICUs) or having complications while in the NICU are also more likely to suffer hearing loss. Around 25% of babies are diagnosed with hearing loss whose etiology is unknown.

Signs of hearing impairment

If an infant does not display a startle response at loud noises, this is a potential sign of hearing loss. This can also indicate other developmental disabilities, but because hearing loss is the most prevalent disability among newborns, hearing screening is a priority. Between birth and 3 or 4 months old, babies should turn toward the source of a sound; if they do not, it could indicate hearing loss. A child who does not utter first words like *mama* or *dada* by age 1 could have hearing impairment. When babies or young children do not turn their heads when their names are called, adults may mistake this for inattention or ignoring; however, children turning upon seeing adults, but not upon hearing their names, can indicate hearing loss. Babies and children who seem to hear certain sounds but not others may have partial hearing losses. Delayed speech-language development or unclear speech, not following directions, saying "Huh?" often, and wanting higher TV or music volumes can indicate hearing loss in children.

Factors that can contribute to speech and language impairment

Some speech and language disorders in children have unknown causes. Others have known causes such as hearing loss: Speech and language are normally acquired primarily through the auditory sense, so children with impaired hearing have delayed and impaired development of speech and language. Brain injuries, neurological disorders, viral diseases, and some medications can also cause problems with developing language or speech.

Children with intellectual disabilities are more likely to have delayed language development, and their speech is also more likely to develop more slowly and to be distorted. Cerebral palsy causes neuromuscular weakness and incoordination of speech. When severe, it can cause inability to produce recognizable speech sounds; some children without speech can still vocalize, and some cannot. A cleft palate or lip and other physical impairments affect speech. Inadequate speech-language modeling at home inhibits speech-language development. Vocal abuse in children (screaming, coughing, throat clearing, or excessive talking) can cause vocal nodules or polyps, causing voice disorders. Stuttering can be related to maturation, anxiety or stress, auditory feedback defects, or unknown causes.

In speech, most phonological disorders are articulatory; that is, children fail to pronounce specific speech sounds or phonemes correctly beyond the normal developmental age for achieving accuracy. Stuttering, disfluency, and rate and rhythm disorders cause children to repeat phonemes, especially initial word sounds; to repeat words; to prolong vowels or consonants; or to block, that is, straining so hard to produce a sound that, pressure builds, but no sound issues. Their speech rates may also speed and slow irregularly. Children with voice disorders can have voices that sound hoarse, raspy, overly nasal, higher- or lower-pitched than normal, overly weak or strident, and whispery or harsh. Hoarseness is common with vocal nodules and polyps. Cleft palate commonly causes hypernasality. In language, one of the most common impairments is delayed language development due to environmental deprivation, intellectual disabilities, neurological damage or defects, hearing loss, visual impairment, and so on. Children with neurological damage or disorders may exhibit aphasias, language disorders characterized by receptive difficulty with understanding spoken or written language, or expressive difficulty constructing spoken or written language.

Physical and health impairments that cause disabling conditions

In the special education field of early childhood education, *other health impairment* is a term referring to health and physical conditions that rob a child of strength, vitality, or alertness or that cause excessive alertness to environmental stimuli, all having the end result of impeding the child's ability to attend or respond to the educational environment. Health problems can be acute, that is short-term or temporary but serious, or chronic, that is, long-term, persistent, or recurrent. Some examples of such health and physical impairments include: cerebral palsy, spina bifida, amputations or missing limbs, muscular dystrophy, cystic fibrosis, asthma, rheumatic fever, sickle-cell anemia, nephritis or kidney disease, leukemia, Tourette syndrome, hemophilia, diabetes, heart disease, AIDS, and lead poisoning. All these conditions and others can interfere with a child's development and ability to attend and learn. In addition to seizure disorders, which often cause neurological damage, seizure-controlling medications also frequently cause drowsiness, interfering with attention and cognition. Attention deficit and attention deficit hyperactivity disorders (ADD and ADHD) limit attention span, focus, and concentration and thus are sometimes classified as health impairments requiring special education services.

Physical and health impairments

The characteristics of children having various physical or health impairments can range from having no limitations to severe limitations in their activities. Children with cerebral palsy, for example, usually have deficiencies in gross and fine motor development and deficits in speech-language development. Physical and health conditions causing severe

- 49 -

debilitation in some children not only seriously limit their daily activities but also cause multiple primary disabilities and impair their intellectual functioning. Other children with physical or health impairments function at average, above-average, or gifted intellectual and academic levels. An important consideration when working with babies and young children having physical or health impairments is handling and positioning them physically. Correctly picking up, holding, carrying, giving assistance, and physically supporting younger children and arranging play materials for them based on their impairment is not only important for preventing injury, pain, and discomfort; it also enables them to receive instruction better and to manipulate materials and perform most efficiently. Preschoolers with physical impairments also tend to have difficulty with communication skills, so educators should give particular attention to facilitating and developing these.

Multiple disabilities

The term *multiple disabilities* refers to any combination of more than 1 disabling condition. For example, a child may be both blind and deaf due to causes such as having rheumatic fever in infancy or early childhood. Anything causing neurological damage before, during, or shortly after birth can result in multiple disabilities, particularly if it is widespread rather than localized. For example, infants deprived of oxygen or suffering traumatic brain injuries in utero, during labor or delivery, or postnatally can sustain severe brain damage. So can babies having encephalitis or meningitis and those whose mothers abused drugs prenatally. Infants with this type of extensive damage can often present with multiple disabilities, including intellectual disabilities, cerebral palsy, physical paralysis, mobility impairment, visual impairment, hearing impairment, and speech-language disorders. They may have any combination of or all of these disabilities as well as others. In addition to a difficulty or inability with normal physical performance, multiply disabled children often have difficulty acquiring and retaining cognitive skills and transferring or generalizing skills among settings and situations.

Developmental delays

Developmental delays can come from genetic or environmental causes or both. Infants and young children with intellectual disabilities are most likely to exhibit developmental delays. Their development generally proceeds similarly to that of normal children but at slower rates; milestones are manifested at later-than-typical ages. Sensory impairments such as with hearing and vision can also delay many aspects of children's development. Children with physical and health impairments are likely to exhibit delays in their motor development and performance of physical activities. Another factor is environmental: Children deprived of adequate environmental stimulation commonly show delays in cognitive, speech-language, and emotional and social development. Children with autism spectrum disorders often have markedly delayed language and speech development; many are nonverbal. Autistic children also typically have impaired social development, caused by and inability or difficulty with understanding others' emotional and social nonverbal communications. When they cannot interpret these, they do not know how to respond and also cannot imitate them; however, they can often learn these skills with special instruction.

Developmental delays mean that a child does not reach developmental milestones at the expected ages. For example, if most babies normally learn to walk between 12 and 15 months of age, a 20-month-old who is not beginning to walk is considered as having a developmental delay. Delays can occur in cognitive, speech-language, social-emotional, gross motor skill, or fine motor skill development. Signs of delayed motor development include stiff or rigid limbs, floppy or limp body posture for the child's age, using 1 side of the body more than the other, and clumsiness unusual for the child's age. Behavioral signs of children's developmental delays include inattention, or shorter than normal attention span for the age; avoiding or infrequent eye contact; focusing on unusual objects for long times or preferring objects over social interaction; excessive frustration when attempting tasks normally simple for children their age; unusual stubbornness; aggressive and acting-out behaviors; daily violent behaviors; rocking; excessive talking to oneself; and not soliciting love or approval from parents.

Traumatic brain injury (TBI)

TBI is defined by the IDEA law (the Individuals with Disabilities Education Act) as "an acquired injury to the brain from external physical force, resulting in total or partial functional disability or psychosocial impairment, or both, that adversely affect a child's educational performance." This definition excludes injuries from birth trauma, congenital injuries, and degenerative conditions. TBI is the foremost cause of death and disability in children (and teens) in the USA. The most common causes of TBI in children include falls, motor vehicle accidents, and physical abuse. In spite of the IDEA's definition, aneurysms and strokes are 3 examples of internal traumas that can also cause TBI in babies and young children. External head injuries that can result in TBI include both open and closed head injuries. Shaken baby syndrome is caused by forcibly shaking an infant. This causes the brain literally to bounce against the insides of the skull, causing rebound injuries, resulting in TBI and even death.

TBI can impair a child's cognitive development and processing. It can impede the language development of children, which is dependent upon cognitive development. Children who have sustained TBI often have difficulties with attention, retention and memory; reasoning, judgment, understanding abstract concepts and thinking abstractly, and problem-solving abilities. TBIs can also impair a child's motor functions and physical abilities. The sensory and perceptual functions of children with TBI can be abnormal. Their ability to process information is often compromised. Their speech can also be affected. In addition, TBIs can impair a child's psychosocial behaviors. Memory deficits are commonest, tend to be more long lasting, and are often area specific; for example, a child may recall personal experiences but not factual information. Other common characteristics of TBI include cognitive inflexibility or rigidity, damaged conceptualization and reasoning, language loss or poor verbal fluency, problems with paying attention and concentrating, inadequate problem solving, and problems with reading and writing.

Prematurity or preterm birth

Babies born before 37 weeks' gestation are classified as premature or preterm. Premature infants can have difficulty with breathing, as their lungs are not fully developed, and with regulating their body temperatures. Premature infants may be born with pneumonia, respiratory distress, extra air or bleeding in the lungs, jaundice, sepsis or infection, hypoglycemia (low blood sugar), severe intestinal inflammation, bleeding into the brain or white-matter brain damage, or anemia. They have lower-than-normal birth weights, body fat, muscle tone, and activity. Additional typical characteristics of premature infants include apnea (interrupted breathing); lanugo (a coating of body hair that full-term infants no longer have); thin, smooth, shiny, translucent skin through which veins are visible; soft, flexible ear cartilage; cryptorchidism (undescended testicles) and small, non-ridged scrotums in males; enlarged clitorises in females; and feeding difficulties caused by weak or defective sucking reflexes or incoordination of swallowing with breathing.

Physicians find it impossible to predict the long-term results of prematurity for any individual baby based on an infant's gestational age and birth weight. However, some related immediate and long-term effects can be identified. Generally, the lower the birth weight and the more prematurely a child is born, the greater the risk is for complications. Infants born at less than 34 weeks of gestation typically cannot coordinate their sucking and swallowing and may temporarily need feeding or breathing tubes or oxygen. They also need special nursery care until able to maintain their body temperatures and weights. Long-term complications of prematurity can include bronchopulmonary dysplasia, a chronic lung condition; delayed physical growth and development; delayed cognitive development; mental or physical delays or disabilities; and blindness, vision loss, or retinopathy of prematurity (formerly called retrolental fibroplasia). While some premature infants sustain long-term disabilities, some severe, other babies born prematurely grow up to show no effects at all; and any results within this range can also occur.

Assessment and Program Planning and Implementation

Tests commonly administered to babies born prematurely

One test that physicians commonly order for premature infants is a blood gas analysis. This test yields the proportions of gases like oxygen, hydrogen, and nitrogen in the blood. Premature infants' organs are not yet fully developed, particularly their lungs and hearts. A major cause of intellectual disabilities and neurological damage is oxygen deprivation, so it is important to ensure sufficient amounts. Tests also assess the baby's blood levels of glucose, calcium, and bilirubin. Glucose is blood sugar, vital for supplying fuel to brain and body systems. Calcium is necessary for proper bone and tooth formation and also for proper conduction of key brain chemicals. Bilirubin is a yellow pigment, a by-product of used red blood cells. The liver makes bile to break down bilirubin, which is then removed from the body through fecal excretion. If the liver cannot do this job adequately, bilirubin builds up in the bloodstream, causing jaundice. It is not uncommon for premature newborns to become jaundiced; this can cause neurological damage if not resolved.

Developmental screenings and evaluations

If a child's development is suspected of being delayed—for example, the child is not reaching developmental milestones during expected age ranges—a developmental screening may be administered. Screening tests are quickly performed and yield more general results. The hospital or doctor's office may give a questionnaire to the parent or caregiver to complete for a screening. Alternatively, a health or education professional may administer a screening test to the child. Screening tests are not intended to diagnose specific conditions or give details; they are meant to identify children who may have some problem. Screenings can overidentify or under-identify developmental delays in children. Hence, if the screening identifies a child as having developmental delay(s), the child is then referred for a developmental evaluation—a much longer, more thorough, comprehensive, in-depth assessment using multiple tests, administered by a psychologist or other highly-trained professional. Evaluation provides a profile of a child's strengths and weaknesses in all developmental domains. Determination of needs for early intervention services or treatment plans is based on evaluation results.

If a young child has been screened for developmental disorders or delays within the past 6 months and no changes have been observed or reported, repeat screening may be waived. Initial screenings are required. Hearing and vision screenings are mandatory in screening young children. Formal developmental measures are also required, which may include screening tests of motor skills development, cognitive development, social-emotional development, and self-help skills development. Formal screening tests of speech-language development are also required. Additional tests recommended during screening include informal measures. For example, checklists, rating scales, and inventories may be used to screen a child's behavior, mood, and performance of motor skills, cognitive skills, self-help skills, and social and emotional skills. On checklists, parents or caregivers check whether the child does or does not demonstrate listed behaviors, or assessors may complete them via parent or caregiver interviews or interviewing and observing the child. Rating scales ask parents, caregivers, and assessors to rate a child's behaviors, affect, mood, and so on, within a range of numbered and labeled descriptions. Inventories list demonstrated skills and needs. Behavioral observations and existing records and information are also used.

Data that a developmental evaluation needs to incorporate

The child's social history should be obtained. This is typically done by a social worker. Details of the child's developmental progress heretofore; the family's composition, socioeconomic status, and situation; and the child's and family's health and medical histories and status should be emphasized. A physician's or nurse's medical assessment is required, including a physical examination, and if indicated, a specialist's examination. A psychologist typically assesses intellectual and cognitive development; at least 1 such test is generally required. At least 1 test of adaptive behavior is also required to assess emotional-social development. Self-help skills are evaluated; this may be included within cognitive, adaptive behavior, or programming assessments. Communication skills are typically evaluated by a speech-language pathologist. Both receptive and expressive language must be tested and comprehensively rather than simply by single-word vocabulary tests. As indicated, speech articulation is also tested. At least 1 test of motor skills, typically administered by a physical or occupational therapist, is required. Programming evaluation requires at least 1 criterion-referenced or curriculum-based measure, typically administered by an educator.

Diagnosing health impairment(s)

A young child, often aged 3 to 5 years, is generally considered to have a health impairment under the following conditions: Developmental testing reveals a delay, for example, of at least 1.5 standard deviations away from the mean or average test scores used as norms for the child's age group in 1 or more of the 5 developmental areas—cognitive, emotional-social, speech-language, gross motor skills, and fine motor skills—and a physician's written statement indicates a specific type of health impairment, any developmental limits it causes, the potential necessity for medication, and medication effects. With the majority of health, medical, and physical impairments, classification of the child's disorder is based on the doctor's diagnosis. However, when attention deficit hyperactivity disorder (ADHD) is found to constitute a disabling health impairment for a child because it interferes with daily functioning, development, and early education, diagnosis is better made via a multidisciplinary team. Differential diagnosis is necessary because ADHD can be confused with or compounded by other conditions.

Diagnosis of attention deficit hyperactivity disorder (ADHD)

When the symptoms of ADHD limit a child's normal development and learning, this condition can be categorized as *other health impairment*. While most health impairments are diagnosed by physicians, ADHD should be diagnosed by multidisciplinary professionals. This is not only because its nature is complex and it involves psychological components such as attention, memory, impulse control, and neurologically based physical hyperactivity. It is also because ADHD can resemble other developmental disorders; it may coexist with them; and the symptoms of each often overlap. Thus, differential diagnosis is important with ADHD. When ADHD is suspected, a comprehensive assessment is indicated, including data obtained from multiple settings, including the home, and evaluations of the child's functioning in the medical, psychological, behavioral, and educational domains. It is also necessary to obtain thorough health and developmental histories of the child.

Multidisciplinary professionals should be involved in differential diagnosis of ADHD due to its multifaceted nature and pervasive effects on child development. The process of evaluation depends on significant components, like the child's specific developmental history, obtained through a combination of parent or caregiver responses, and professional practitioners' findings, and on information obtained via ratings made by teachers and teachers' informal reports of problems observed with the child's behavior and pre-academic functioning within his or her natural environment. Common observational descriptions of children having ADHD include characteristics of impulsivity, inattention, distractibility, and excessive motor, physical, or vocal and verbal activity. Another general set of criteria is that, if multiple observers in different contexts report problematic behaviors by the child, if these problem behaviors started early in childhood, and if the behaviors have existed for longer than 6 months, an eventual diagnosis of ADHD is more likely. Physical examination does not directly contribute to diagnosing ADHD but is necessary to rule out other medical conditions that may mimic or resemble ADHD.

Experts have found that neurological examinations, such as EEG (electroencephalogram), CAT (computer-assisted tomography) scan, PET (positron emission tomography) scan, MRI (magnetic resonance imaging), or fMRI (functional MRI), do not help diagnose or treat ADHD and are only indicated for seizure disorders or other neurological symptoms observed through the child's history and medical and physical examinations. Also, a number of other conditions can produce symptoms similar to those caused by ADHD. For example, some medications cause side effects, including inattention and hyperactivity. Various social and emotional variables can cause a child to experience anxiety, which can have symptoms of distractibility, impulsivity, inattentiveness, or hyperactivity. Sensory impairments can cause the appearance of inattention: The child may be unable to detect sensory stimuli rather than ignoring them. Some systemic medical illnesses can also produce symptoms resembling those of ADHD. Some children with seizure disorders but not ADHD may exhibit ADHD-like symptoms of inattention or distraction, which are really minor (petit-mal or absence) seizure activity. Lead poisoning or other environmental toxicity also can produce symptoms appearing similar to those of ADHD.

While the chief symptoms associated with ADHD are inattentiveness, impulsive behavior, distractibility, and excessive physical activity, there is considerable variation among individual children having ADHD. For example, the degree of severity of this condition can vary widely from one child to the next. In addition, each child can vary in how much he or she exhibits each of these primary characteristics. Some children might not appear to behave very impulsively but show severe deficits in attention. Some may focus better, but only for short periods, and are very easily distracted. Some display very disruptive behavior, while others do not but may daydream excessively, not attending to programming. In general, children who have ADHD can show deficits in following rules and directions. Also, when their developmental skills are evaluated or observed, they are likely to demonstrate inconsistencies in performance over time. To identify or select specific intervention methods and strategies, professionals should use a comprehensive evaluation to obtain information about the child's specific behaviors in his or her natural environment that need remediation.

Collaborative approaches in school districts for screening for special developmental needs

Historically, the tradition was to conduct kindergarten screenings of children entering schools around age 5. However, in recent years, school districts have developed community referral networks to assist in the processes of Child Find, screening, evaluation, and referral for early intervention and early childhood special education and related services. Current models are more informal, proactive, and collaborative. Cooperative educational interagency service efforts give parents information about normal early childhood development and available community resources and offer opportunities for developmental screenings of their young children. Specific procedures are governed by individual U.S. state laws. Generally, district networks implementing current models send developmental review forms to parents to complete in advance, and then they attend a developmental screening at a community site. Parents discuss normal early childhood growth and development with program staff, while in the same room, trained professionals observe their children as they play. Children's vision and hearing are also screened. Parents can discuss their children's current development with psychologists, early childhood educators, or counselors. Thereafter, they can learn about community resources.

Child Find

Child Find is an ongoing process with the aim of locating, identifying, and referring young children with disabilities and their families as early as possible for service programs. This process consists of activities designed to raise public awareness and screenings and evaluations to identify and diagnose disabilities. The federal IDEA law mandates under Part B that disabled children are guaranteed early childhood special education services and under Part C that infants and toddlers at risk for developmental delays are guaranteed early intervention programs. (Eligibility guidelines vary by U.S. states.) The IDEA requires school districts to find, identify, and evaluate children with disabilities in their attendance areas. School districts have facilitated this Child Find process by establishing community informed referral networks whose members refer children who may have exceptional educational needs (EENs). Network members typically include parents, doctors, birth-to-3 programs, child care programs, Head Start programs, public health agencies, social service agencies, and any other community members with whom the young children come into contact.

Typically, school districts track screening locations, districts involved, participants, and screening frequencies by area, numbers and ages of children screened, and referrals. For example, as identifying information, a district's data collection form may include the screening county; school district(s) or Child and Family Connection(s) (CFCs) responsible for screening and working with a screening entity; the screening date, and for cumulative reporting purposes, the screening month; the place(s) of the screening event(s); the individual in charge of each screening session, the contact person and his or her contact information; any agency or agencies or individual provider(s) that conduct the screening activities; and the agency or provider type. The total number of children screened during an event or cumulative monthly report, and number by each age, are recorded for tracking. Numbers of children referred for further evaluation, aged 0 to 3 and 3 to 5+ respectively, are recorded as are referral types and agency names. The numbers of children passing screening but referred for rescreening for various reasons (e.g., the child could not screen, parents reported variable functioning, the screener had specific concerns, etc.) may also be recorded.

A comprehensive Child Find system includes at least: a definition of the target population, public awareness, referral and intake, screening and identification of young children who may be eligible for services under the IDEA (the Individuals with Disabilities Education Act), eligibility determination, tracking, and interagency coordination. Early Intervention programs provide special services for infants and toddlers from birth through 2 years old and their families. These services are designed to identify and serve the needs of children these ages having developmental disorders or delays or at risk for having them in the areas of physical, cognitive, emotional, social, communicative, and adaptive development according to the IDEA. Individual states and territories determine their respective policies for complying with IDEA provisions. Some of the services typically provided in early intervention programs include: assistive technology services and devices, audiology and hearing services, family training and counseling, educational programs, evaluative and diagnostic medical services, health services to allow the child to benefit from other services, nursing services, nutritional services, occupational therapy, physical therapy, psychological services, respite care services, speech-language services, transportation, and service coordination services.

Eligibility determination for services under the IDEA (the Individuals with Disabilities Education Act)

The federal IDEA law's Part C mandates and broadly describes early intervention services for children aged 0 to 2 with developmental disabilities but assigns specific definitions and eligibility criteria to individual states. IDEA Part C requires states and jurisdictions to serve (1) children with developmental delays and (2) children with diagnosed mental or physical conditions putting them at high risk for developmental delays. States and jurisdictions also have the option to provide services to children at risk of significant developmental delays through not receiving early intervention. Defining eligible populations and establishing eligibility criteria affect types and numbers of children who need or get services, types of services rendered, and early intervention expenses, challenging state governments. While many states wanted to serve at-risk children after IDEA established its Early Intervention Program, fear of costs limited how many states included them in their definitions. Some states do not serve, but monitor, at-risk children and refer them if developmental delays appear.

The IDEA Part C specifies the areas of development that states must include in defining developmental delays. However, individual states must identify the criteria they use to determine eligibility, including pertinent diagnostic instruments, procedures, and functional levels. States currently use quantitative and qualitative measures. Quantitative criteria for developmental delay include: difference between chronological age and performance level, expressed as a percentage of chronological age; performance at a given number of months below chronological age; or number of standard deviations (SDs) below mean of performance on a norm-referenced test. Qualitative criteria include: development considered atypical or delayed for established norms or observed behaviors considered atypical. At least 1 state differentially defines delay according to a child's age in months, with the rationale that a 25% delay, for example, is very different for a 1-year-old than a 3-year-old. Quantitative criteria for defining delay and determining eligibility vary widely among states. A 25% or 20% delay; 2 SDs below mean in 1+ areas or 1.5 SD below mean in 2+ areas are some common state criteria.

Many U.S. states quantitatively express developmental delays in children aged 0 to 2 years through standard deviations below the mean on standardized, norm-referenced tests; percentage of the chronological age; or developmental age in months. However, some areas of child development are not well described by these methods. Another consideration is that traditional standardized assessment instruments may vary across developmental domains or children's ages. To address these concerns, some states also include qualitative data, like observations of atypical behaviors, along with quantitative measures to determine developmental delays. Additional considerations with using traditional testing instruments are that not enough such instruments exist for the 0 to 2 years age group; and those that do exist do not have good predictive validity. Hence, the IDEA's Part C regulations also require informed clinical opinion as a basis for determining eligibility. Such opinion is usually obtained through multidisciplinary consensus including parents, multiple data sources, and quantitative and qualitative data. Several states only identify informed clinical opinion, without separate quantitative criteria, as their eligibility criterion.

In applying IDEA's Part C early intervention provisions for children aged 0 to 2 years, many states divide risk into established risk, biological or medical risk, and environmental risk. Established risk is a "diagnosed physical or mental condition which has a high probability of resulting in developmental delay." This includes genetic, chromosomal, or congenital disorders; severe hearing, vision, or other sensory impairments; innate metabolic disorders; congenital infections; disorders reflecting disturbed nervous system development; fetal alcohol syndrome; other disorders secondary to exposure to toxins; and severe attachment disorders. Part C makes these eligible regardless of the presence or absence of measured delay. Several states add many other conditions to this definition. Biological or medical risk includes low birth weight, chronic lung disease, intraventricular hemorrhage at birth, and failure to thrive. Because these do not always cause DD, comprehensive evaluation by multidisciplinary teams (MDTs) must determine eligibility and specific services. Environmental risk includes poverty, homelessness, parental age, education, DD, substance abuse, family social disorganization, and child abuse or neglect. Eligibility and service determination in this category require MDT evaluation as with biological or medical risk.

Scientists find that developmental outcomes for children are not reliably predicted by any 1 risk factor or event. Developmental risk increases with increased biological, medical, or environmental risk factors. However, researchers have found some variables that afford resiliency in children to offset risk factors. These can include the child's basic temperament, the child having high self-esteem, the child having a good emotional relationship with at least 1 parent; and the child having experiences of successful learning. These findings indicate that assessments should include criteria for multiple biological and environmental risk factors, for cumulative biological and environmental risk factors, and for protective or resilience factors, considering all of these in the context of change occurring over time. Under the IDEA (the Individuals with Disabilities Education Act), U.S. states have the option to provide early intervention services to children considered at risk for adverse developmental outcomes as well as those already identified with them. Some states apply multiple-risk models, requiring 3 to 5 risk factors for service eligibility. Some states also determine eligibility with less DD when biological, medical, or environmental risk factors also exist.

Even if preschoolers are not yet enrolled in the public school system, the IDEA charges school districts with providing them evaluations, eligibility determinations, and services.

Parents need not pay for evaluations, which are funded by federal and state governments. If a child is determined eligible for early intervention or early childhood special education services, these are also provided by school districts at no cost to parents. In every state, parent training and information courses and community parent resource centers are funded by the federal government. For rural families, the goals of early intervention and early special education services are the same as in urban settings; however, services may be delivered differently. Organizations like the University of Montana Rural Institute and the National Rural Education Association can provide rural families with information about services. Special-needs Native American infants, toddlers, and children living on reservations are included under state lead agencies' responsibilities for providing early intervention services and state education agencies' responsibilities for special education services to preschoolers.

Intervention and preschool special education services for special needs children of U.S. military families

Military families stationed both in the United States and overseas who have young special needs children can seek information and assistance from the federally funded organization Specialized Training of Military Families (STOMP). The staff of STOMP is composed of parents having special needs children themselves, who also have been trained to work with other parents of special needs children. STOMP staff members are spouses of military personnel who thus understand the unique, specialized circumstances and needs of military families. Another government agency, the U.S. Department of Defense, includes the office of the Department of Defense Education Activity (DoDEA) and provides comprehensive guidance to military families with special needs children who are eligible to receive, or are receiving, free appropriate public education (FAPE) as mandated by the IDEA law (the Individuals with Disabilities Education Act), whether that education is located in the United States or in other countries.

Assessing learning progress and achievement

To plan and implement instruction, to evaluate its effectiveness, and to monitor children's progress toward program goals, ECE teachers must assess children's development and learning. Instruction and assessment should be mutual; that is, assessments evaluate what instruction is developing, and instruction develops what is being assessed. Assessment must have validity (it measures what it is meant to measure) and reliability (it can be reproduced with the same results). It should not be used for tracking, labeling, or other practices detrimental to children. It should be purposeful, strategic, and continual. Its results inform communications with children's families, instructional planning and implementation, and evaluations and improvements of programs' and teachers' effectiveness. It should focus on progress toward developmentally and educationally important goals. Programs should have systems for gathering, interpreting, and applying formative assessment results to guide classroom activity. Teachers must continually make assessments, including during all interactions with children, to improve instruction and learning.

ECE assessment methods are appropriate for young children's developmental levels and experiences, acknowledge individual student differences, and accordingly permit various ways for students to demonstrate competence. Hence, appropriate ECE classroom assessment methods include clinical interviews, teacher observations of children, portfolio assessments and collections of work samples produced by children, and records of children's performance during authentic (real-life or close to it) instructional activities. Assessment tests not only children's independent achievements but also performance of tasks with needed scaffolding (temporary support), as with groups, pairs, or other assistance. Teachers incorporate information from families and children themselves about their work, along with teacher evaluations, for overall assessment. Assessments are designed for specific purposes; proven to yield valid, reliable results for those; and only used for those purposes. Major decisions for children, like enrollment or placement, are always based on multiple data sources, never 1 instrument. Sources include observations by and interactions with parents and family, teachers, and specialists. If screening or assessment identifies possible special needs, follow-up, evaluation, and referral as needed are made appropriately without immediate diagnosis or labeling.

Individualized Family Service Plan (IFSP)

When a child aged from birth through 2 years has been screened, referred for comprehensive evaluation to determine whether he or she has a disability eligible for early intervention services under the IDEA law Individualized Family Service Plan, and through the evaluation results, found eligible, the next step is to develop an IFSP. This is a written document that describes in detail what early intervention services the child will be receiving. The IFSP is guided by certain principles, including that the young child's needs are closely attached to his or her family's needs and that the family is the child's most important resource. Therefore, supporting the family and building upon the family's particular strengths are the best ways to meet the needs of and support the child. The IFSP is created by a multidisciplinary team that includes the parents and is a plan for the whole family. Other interagency team members, depending on the child's needs, may include medical personnel, therapists, social workers, child development specialists, and so on.

An IFSP is developed for children 0 to 2 years determined eligible through evaluation results for early intervention services. It must include: the child's current levels of functioning and needs in physical, cognitive, communication, emotional, social, and adaptive development; with parental consent, family information including the parents' and other close family members' concerns, priorities, and resources; primary effects of the IFSP expected for the child and family; specific services to be delivered; where the child will receive services in natural environments, like at home, in the community, elsewhere, or a combination; if services will not be in the natural environment, a rationale justifying this; specific service times and locations; number of sessions or days for services and session durations; whether services will be 1:1 or in groups; who will pay for the services; the name of the service coordinator managing IFSP implementation; steps supporting future transition from early intervention to other programs and services; and optionally, other services of interest to the family, for example, finances, raising children with disabilities, and so on.

When infants and toddlers are determined eligible for IDEA (the Individuals with Disabilities Education Act) services, parents and professionals from multiple, relevant disciplines develop an IFSP for services to family and child. Professionals must thoroughly explain the plan to parents, and parents must give informed, written consent before the child receives services. Every U.S. state has its own set of IFSP guidelines. The service coordinator can explain state guidelines to parents. Early intervention services range from simple to complex, including things such as prescribing eyeglasses, special instruction, home visits, counseling, and family training to help meet the child's special needs. Some services are provided in the family's home and some in hospitals, local health departments, community day care centers, clinics, or other settings. Natural environments, that is, settings where the child normally lives, plays, and learns are preferred. Personnel delivering services must be qualified. Both public and private agencies may be involved in service delivery.

The IDEA provides that, if a child has a qualifying disability, is at risk for developmental delay or disability, or is suspected of having an eligible disability, families must be given Child Find services, developmental screenings, assessment referrals, comprehensive evaluations, a developed and reviewed IFSP in which parents participate, and service coordination all at no cost to the family. Whether families pay for services other than those named above is determined by each U.S. state's individual policies. Some services can be covered by Medicaid, by private health insurance policies, or for Native American families, by Indian Health Services. Some service providers may charge fees to families on a sliding scale basis according to the family's earned income so that lower-income families can afford them. The law provides that an eligible child cannot be denied special services simply because his or her family cannot afford to pay for them; providers must make all efforts to deliver services to all babies and toddlers needing assistance and support.

Inclusive Learning Environments

Special education services for preschool children aged 3 to 5 years

Special education for preschoolers is education specifically designed to meet the individual needs of a child aged 3 to 5 years with a disability or developmental delay. The specialized design of this instruction can include adaptations to the content, to the teaching methods, and the way instruction is delivered to meet a disabled child's unique needs. Special education for preschoolers includes various settings, such as in the home, in classrooms, hospitals, institutions, and others. It also includes a range of related services, such as speech-language pathology services, specialized physical education instruction, early vocational training, and training in travel skills. The school district's special education system provides evaluation and services to eligible preschoolers free of charge. Evaluation's purposes are to determine whether a child has a disability under the IDEA's (the Individuals with Disabilities Education Act) definitions and determine that child's present educational needs.

If parents observe that their preschooler is not attaining developmental milestones within the expected age ranges or does not seem to be developing in the same way as most other children, they should seek evaluation for possible developmental delay or disability. Although 3- to-5-year-olds are likely not in elementary school yet, the elementary school in a family's school district is still the best first contact because the IDEA law (the Individuals with Disabilities Education Act) specifies that school districts must provide special education services at no family cost to eligible children, including preschoolers. Another excellent source of more information about special education is the National Dissemination Center for Children with Disabilities (NICHCY) of the U.S. Department of Education's Office of Special Education Programs. They partner with nonprofit organizations like the Academy for Educational Development (AED) to produce useful documents for families with special needs children. NICHCY supplies state resource sheets listing main contacts regarding special education services in each U.S. state. Families can obtain these sheets at NICHCY's website or by telephone.

Under the IDEA (the Individuals with Disabilities Education Act), evaluation information sources include: physicians' reports, the child's medical history, developmental test results, current classroom observations and assessments (when applicable), completed developmental and behavioral checklists, feedback and observations from parents and all other members of the evaluation team, and any other significant records, reports, and observations regarding the child. Under the IDEA, involved in the evaluation are parents, at least 1 regular education teacher and special education teacher if the child has these, and any special education service provider working with the child—for children receiving early intervention services from birth through age 2 and transitioning to preschool special education, it may be an early intervention service provider; a school administrator knowledgeable about children with disabilities, special education policies, regular education curriculum, and resources available; a psychologist or educator who can interpret evaluation results and discuss indicated instruction; individuals with special expertise or knowledge regarding the child (recruited by school or parents); when appropriate, the child; and other professionals, for example, physical or occupational therapists, speech therapists, medical specialists, and so on.

Individualized Education Program (IEP) goals and objectives for preschoolers aged 3 to 5

In an IEP, the goals are more global, describing a skill for the child to acquire or a task to master. The objectives are more specific articulations of achievements that will demonstrate the child's mastery of the goal. For example, if a goal is for the child to increase his or her functional communicative vocabulary, a related objective might be for the child to acquire X number of new words in X length of time; another related objective could be for the child to use the words acquired in 90% of recorded relevant situations. If the goal is for the child to demonstrate knowledge and discrimination of colors, 1 objective might be for the child to identify correctly a red, yellow, and blue block 95% of the time when asked to point out each color within a group of blocks. Progress toward or achievement of some objectives may be measured via formal tests; with preschoolers, many others are measured via observational data collection.

After a preschool child is evaluated, the parents and involved school personnel meet to discuss the evaluation results. Parents are included in the group that decides whether the child is eligible for special education services based on those results. For eligible children, the parents and school personnel will develop an IEP. Every child who will receive special education services must have an IEP. The main purposes of the IEP are (1) to establish reasonable educational goals for the individual child and (2) to indicate what services the school district will provide to the child. The IEP includes a statement of the child's present levels of functioning and performance. It also includes a list of more general instructional goals for the child to achieve through school and parental support along with more specific learning objectives reflecting those goals and specifying exactly what the child will be able to demonstrate, under what circumstances, how much of the time—for example, a percentage of recorded instances—and within what time period (e.g., 1 year).

School multidisciplinary team (MDT)

While the new school or preschool is waiting for records to arrive from a transferring child's previous program, if the MDT has been informed that the child has already had an IEP developed and in place, the team should not place the child in a special education class or group in the interim, which would be premature and inappropriate without first having the prior school's records and conducting a team meeting to ascertain the child's instructional needs. Federal regulations provide that making an interim placement that is, placing the child in a regular education class or program, is more appropriate until the child's records are received and further, more detailed information is available. If the child already has an IEP, then a comprehensive evaluation was conducted to determine his or her special education eligibility. Therefore, the team should not duplicate this by performing another complete evaluation, consuming unnecessary time and resources.

Transdisciplinary Play-Based Assessment (TPBA)

TPBA is Transdisciplinary Play-Based Assessment. Very young children have not developed the cognitive skills needed to respond to many formal assessment instruments. For example, you would not ask a 3-year-old to conjugate verbs, add several single-digit numbers, or count more than a few concrete objects. This is true even of normally developing young children and even more so of those with developmental disabilities whose cognitive development may not be at typical age levels. However, most young children naturally engage in and enjoy playing. TPBA takes advantage of this by having trained professionals observe a young child at play. Together with parents' input, the observers can determine the child's performance levels of many motor, cognitive, adaptive, emotional, and social skills. Typically, a TPBA team collaborating or consulting with parents would include personnel such as a speech-language pathologist, a psychologist, a teacher, and a physical or occupational therapist. These specialists are most familiar with child skills across all domains of development that can be directly observed during play.

Activity-based intervention for young children

Activity-based intervention is (1) child directed, (2) embeds intervention across varied activities, (3) utilizes naturally and logically occurring antecedents (events coming before a desired behavior) and consequences (events immediately following a desired behavior), and (4) focuses on developing functional skills. For example, if a young child demonstrates particular interest in balloons, activity-based intervention using balloons in activities fulfills component (1) of being child directed. The teacher might elicit the child's requests for balloons, give directions for the child to follow in painting or decorating balloons, teach words related to balloons and have the child use them, and offer the child games to play with balloons. This fulfills component (2) of embedding intervention across varied activities. Component (3) of natural and logical antecedents and consequences is met by using balloons, which are naturally motivating and rewarding to this child. The activities named all develop functional skills (4): requesting desired objects, following directions, fine motor skills, vocabulary development and application, and learning and following (game) rules.

Premack principle

The Premack principle is a principle derived from behaviorism or learning theory. It involves encouraging a child to engage in a behavior less desirable to him or her by making a behavior more desirable or rewarding to the child contingent upon demonstrating the less desired behavior. Behaviorism has established that people (and animals) are more likely to repeat any behavior that receives a reward, or reinforcement, immediately after it occurs. Adults are more likely to repeat work tasks when they are paid money for them; children are more likely to eat their vegetables when they receive dessert for doing so. For example, if Johnny loves to play with finger paints but will only tolerate wearing the headphones that are an important part of his educational programming (and do not cause discomfort) for 1 to 2 minutes at a time, contingent reinforcement could be used to increase this time by letting him have finger paints only after progressively longer periods wearing the headphones—2 minutes, then 3, then 5, and so on.

Progress monitoring, updating, and revising Individualized Education Programs (IEPs) for young children

Once a child has been identified with a disability, determined eligible for special education and related services under the IDEA (the Individuals with Disabilities Education Act), and had an IEP developed and implemented, the child's progress must be monitored. Monitoring methods may be related to evaluation methods. For example, if a child identified with problem behaviors was initially evaluated using a behavioral checklist, school personnel can use the same checklist periodically, comparing its results to the baseline levels of frequency and severity originally obtained. If an affective disorder or disturbance was

- 64 -

identified and instruments like the Beck Depression Inventory or Anxiety Inventory were used, these can be used again periodically; reduced symptoms would indicate progress. If progress with IEP goals and objectives is less or greater than expected, the IEP team meets and may revise the program. This can include specifying shorter or longer times to achieve some goals and objectives; lowering or raising requirements proving too difficult or easy; resetting successive objective criteria in smaller or larger increments; changing teaching methods, content, or materials used, and so on.

Response to Intervention (RTI), Positive Behavior Support/Positive Behavioral Interventions and Supports (PBS/PBIS)

Response to Intervention (RTI), Positive Behavior Support/Positive Behavioral Interventions and Supports (PBS/PBIS), and other service delivery models are very similar. They are generally implemented school-wide, program-wide, or classroom-wide depending on the educational program; many schools use these approaches on a school-wide basis based on the philosophy of proactively preventing learning problems by providing positive support. These models consist of tiers of gradually increasing support along a continuum. Numbers of tiers may vary, but a common feature is using 3 tiers. For example, the first tier is called primary intervention and implements systems that apply to all students, settings, and staff. This tier generally applies to around 80% of the students in a school, program, or classroom. The second tier is called secondary intervention and involves specialized group systems for students identified as at risk, generally involving about 15% of students. The third tier, tertiary intervention, uses specialized, individualized systems for students with intensive needs, usually about 5% of student populations.

In 3-tiered service delivery models, Tier 1 targets all students for support to meet the needs of the general student population and prevent problems before they occur. In Tier 1, general education teachers deliver core instructional programs that are based on solid research evidence to students. While this entails reading, writing, and mathematics for school-age students, for preschoolers it involves pre-academic skills like phonological awareness, alphabetic awareness, vocabulary development, counting skills using concrete objects, categorizing objects, and adaptive skills development for functioning independently in daily life. Student progress is monitored using measurements based on the given curriculum. The results of student progress monitoring are analyzed to identify students who are not making sufficient progress and are therefore at risk for developmental delays or learning problems. Students thus identified as at risk would qualify for Tier 2 intervention.

While Tier 1 in 3-tier models addresses all students and is meant to meet typical student needs, Tier 2 is designed with additional instruction to help at-risk children to attain expected grade-level skills when they fall behind with Tier 1 instruction. Tier 2 interventions are generally supplemental instruction in small groups, with teacher-student ratios of up to 1:5, usually lasting 8 to 12 weeks and administered by special education teachers, specialists, or tutors. Programs, procedures, and teaching strategies in Tier 2 support Tier 1 instruction as well as supplementing and enhancing it. Tier 2 focuses on research evidence-based practices found effective for at-risk children. Students are introduced to Tier 2 as soon as possible after Tier 1 student progress monitoring determines they have fallen behind grade levels. This benefits many students, such as with specific learning disabilities, in bypassing lengthy referral and evaluation procedures otherwise required for special education. Monitoring showing sufficient progress dictates a return to general education classrooms; insufficient progress leads to another round of Tier 2 intervention.

Children who fall behind in general Tier 1 instruction designed to support all or most students are placed in Tier 2, where supplemental instruction is given, providing additional support to children at risk for developmental delays, disorders, or learning problems. When progress monitoring finds a student is not making adequate progress toward grade levels after 2 rounds of Tier 2 intervention, or whose progress is severely limited in 1 round of Tier 2, Tier 3 intervention is indicated. Tier 3 involves instruction customized for the individual child; provides much more intensive, sustained support; and depending on the student's needs, can have much longer durations than Tier 2 interventions. Typically, instruction is in smaller groups with teacher-student ratios of no more than 1:3. Progress monitoring is closer and more ongoing in Tier 3. If a child meets the program's established benchmarks as determined by monitoring or testing, he or she may be exited to Tier 1. However, if the student then fails without such intensive support, he or she may be returned to Tier 2 or Tier 3.

RTI models (and Positive Behavioral Support [PBS] models, which are very similar) generally use 3 tiers of instructional intervention. Tier 1 applies to all students, meets most student needs, and can prevent problems through proactive support. Students failing to meet grade-level expectations in Tier 1 are placed in Tier 2 to receive specialized supplemental instruction in smaller groups from a qualified specialist, special education teacher, or tutor. If this is ineffective, Tier 3 provides more intensive support, individualized to each student, in even smaller groups. Some educators recommend a 4-step process in a protocol treatment approach to RTI: (1) screening, involving Tier 1 or all students—responsibility is shared by general and special education teachers; (2) implementing general education and monitoring responses to it involves Tier 1—general education departments and teachers are responsible for this; (3) implementing supplementary, diagnostic instructional trials and monitoring responses involves Tier 2—responsibility is shared by general and special education teachers; (4) designating and classifying disability, special intensive instructional placement, and monitoring thereof affect Tier 3—special education professionals are responsible.

Movement from simpler to more complex abilities relative to cognitive and emotional skills

Increasing complexity is a principle throughout child development observed in nearly all domains including motor and physical, linguistic, cognitive, and social skills. Neurological development enables growing children to use their expanding memories and organizational abilities to combine simpler routines they have learned into more complex strategies. Even preschoolers understand some abstract concepts, such as that addition creates more while subtraction creates fewer and the one-to-one principle in counting things. However, children proceed in general from more concrete to more abstract thought as they grow. Children also progress from infancy's complete dependence to learning control and internalizing it, and adults play important parts in helping them. When babies are aroused and adults soothe them, this helps them learn to self-soothe. When preschool teachers provide scaffolding and support for dramatic role-plays, help young children learn how to express their feelings, and involve them in planning and decision making, they help them develop emotional self-regulation, to maintain focused attention, and to manage strong feelings.

Constructivist and interactionist orientations to child cognitive development

Constructivism states that young children build their comprehension and knowledge of reality through their experiences with the environment and interactions with family, peers, older children, teachers, and media. Through manipulating concrete objects and learning abstract concepts, children form hypotheses regarding the world and test these via interacting with things, people, and their own thinking processes. They observe events, reflect on their discoveries, imagine possibilities, ask questions, and form answers. Such owning of knowledge by children affords deeper comprehension and superior generalization and application of learning to different contexts. Variation in children's learning needs dictates variation in teaching methods. In both play and structured activities, teachers having wide ranges of strategies can choose the best one for each particular situation, context, learning goal, and individual child needs at the moment. This includes providing greater support, even during play or exploration, to children needing it. It also encompasses teacher demonstration and modeling, providing challenges, specific instruction, and directions, and organizing classrooms and planning to further education goals through opportunities presented in child- and teacher-initiated activities.

Vygotsky's Zone of Proximal Development (ZPD) and Bruner's scaffolding

What Vygotsky termed the ZPD is the area wherein children best learn skills just beyond their current mastery levels and accomplish learning tasks which they could not achieve alone through guidance and support from adults and from other children with slightly higher skill levels. Scaffolding is Bruner's related term for support that adults provide to learning children as needed and gradually withdraw as the child's competence increases until the child can complete a task or skill independently. When achieving autonomy in this manner, children can also generalize, applying skills learned to various new contexts. An important consideration for educators to maintaining children's motivation and persistence is enabling their success at new tasks more often than not. Most children give up trying after repeatedly failing. Another educator consideration is repeatedly giving children opportunities for practicing and consolidating new concepts and skills. This allows the mastery children need to apply and generalize learning. Educators need knowledge of child developmental sequences, plus close observation of individual children's thought processes, to provide challenges without frustration.

Creating a caring learning community

Children learn about themselves and their environments through observation of and participation in the learning community. By demonstrating that each member of the community values and is valued by other members, educators help children learn to establish constructive relationships with others. They also help them learn to value each individual and to recognize and respect all individual and group differences. Because a significant context wherein children develop and learn is relationships with adults and peers, educators can give them various opportunities to play with others, have conversations and discussions with peers and adults, and collaborate on projects and investigations to promote development and learning. By assigning young children to small groups, educators can give them opportunities to learn and practice social interaction; cooperation in problem solving, sharing and building upon each other's ideas; and expanding their thinking. Such interactions support young children's construction of their understandings of reality through their interactions with other members of the learning community.

Planning and implementing EC instruction relative to program curriculum goals

1. ECE teachers are responsible for knowing what their program's learning goals are and how their program's curriculum is designed for attaining these goals. They implement their program's curriculum by teaching young children using practices that fit the general developmental sequences wherein children learn certain skills and concepts that build upon children's prior knowledge, understanding, and experience and, additionally, which are most responsive to the abilities and needs of the individual children that they are teaching.
2. ECE teachers plan learning experiences for young children that are effective in implementing a comprehensive curriculum. One aim in teaching such a comprehensive curriculum is to help young children to achieve the most important learning goals across the physical, cognitive, social, and emotional domains. Another objective is to teach preschoolers basic skills that will prepare them for later school success across all academic disciplines, for example, language literacy, including English as a second language, math, sciences, arts and music, social studies, health, and physical education.

Planning environments, schedules, and activities

By offering richly varied ideas, challenges, and materials, ECE teachers can provide young children with firsthand activities that give them creatively and intellectually stimulating experiences that invite children's ongoing, active engagement, exploration, and investigation. During periods of child-initiated or child-chosen activity, teachers can help and guide children not yet able to put such activities to good use or enjoy them. They can also support children more able to choose by giving them opportunities to make meaningful choices and decisions. Effective ECE teachers organize daily and weekly schedules to afford children substantial time periods for uninterrupted play, exploration, investigation, and social interaction with peers and adults. ECE teachers should also arrange experiences and interactions and provide materials for young children that allow them fully to push the boundaries of their imaginations and of their linguistic, self-regulatory, and interactional abilities to practice the skills that they have newly developed.

Assuring full participation, development, and learning

ECE teachers can encourage young children to select and plan their own learning activities, which helps them develop initiative. Teachers can ask children questions, pose problems, and make suggestions and comments to stimulate their thinking and expand their learning. To expand the scope of children's interests and thoughts, teachers can introduce stimulating ideas, problems, hypotheses, or problems, and experiences novel to them. In adjusting activity complexity for children's knowledge and skill levels, teachers increase challenges commensurately with children's increasing understanding and competency. Providing experiences with genuine challenge and success is a way teachers can enhance children's motivation, persistence, risk taking, confidence, and competence as learners. Intensive interviews, extended conversation and discourse, and similar strategies encouraging children to revisit and reflect upon their experiences are ways teachers can further children's conceptual understanding. ECE teachers should also give specific feedback (e.g.,

"You got the same total both times you counted those buttons!") rather than generic praises (e.g., "Good job!").

Providing more intensive, enriched, and expanded learning experiences

1. Teachers must be careful not to put additional pressure on children beginning school with disadvantages. This can discourage and frustrate them, preventing them from having the opportunity to enjoy learning and be successful at it.
2. Teachers must use the available time with high intentionality to enable children from disadvantaged backgrounds to make the best learning progress. Teachers should focus on the most important skills and competencies these children need to develop. They provide experiences that they find are most engaging to the children to help them attain these needed skills.
3. ECE teachers realize that play experiences of a high quality confer benefits to children by affording learning and practice in emotional self-regulation and language use, and they develop and exercise cognitive skills and social skills. Realizing this, teachers do not restrict or decrease disadvantaged children's opportunities to play. Rather, they model elements of mature, rich play and provide children with needed scaffolding and support for them to apply these elements in their own play.

Making learning experiences responsive and accessible to all children

In making learning responsive and accessible to all children's needs, ECE teachers must include those learning English as a new language, those from diverse cultures, those having disabilities, and those in impoverished and otherwise difficult living situations. To do this, teachers use a wide range of materials, equipment, teaching strategies, and experiences to address individual differences in children's previous experiences, developmental levels, abilities, skills, interests, and needs. They include each child's home language and culture into the learning community, such that the child's home and family ties are supported and the community realizes and values each culture and language's unique contributions. They include all children in all activities and model and encourage children's behaviors and peer interactions to be inclusive. ECE teachers can meet the needs of children with disabilities using their own strategies, plus consulting as needed with family and indicated specialists, and ensure children receive necessary adaptations or modifications and specialized services to succeed in learning.

Achievement gaps associated with the socioeconomic and ethnic status of young children and families in America

Research finds that, in comparing standardized measures of academic achievement, low-income Hispanic and African-American children fall behind their peers significantly and encounter more difficulties in school settings throughout the school years. Children's early access to quality schools and programs differs dramatically across socioeconomic and ethnic groups, as do their early educational experiences. Disparity between minority children's home cultures and school cultures is a factor. Also, young children's exposure to language is basic to literacy development, cognitive development, and learning; the home linguistic experiences of many low-income children are substantially less rich than those of middle-class children. Children in low-income families hear dramatically fewer words and are involved in fewer extended conversations with parents and other family members. One example of the results of these differences is that significant socioeconomic disparities in children's vocabulary knowledge are found by the time they are 3 years old.

Typically, children from less educated or more impoverished families are found to begin school with lower levels of basic skills in language, reading, and mathematics. Children from the lowest socioeconomic group begin kindergarten with scores on cognitive measures averaging 60% lower than the most affluent socioeconomic group. African-American children have 21% lower average math achievement, and Hispanic children 19% lower, than white children. This is mainly because of the socioeconomic status of these ethnic groups. Additionally, entrenched inequities in communities and hence in schools make these early gaps in achievement more likely to increase with time than to decrease. Concern about achievement gaps among U.S. demographic groups is contained within a larger concern about competing in a global economy: Comparing standardized test scores shows that America's students have not consistently exceeded or matched student achievements in other industrialized countries. Such concern has fueled the accountability and standards movement, as exemplified by the 2001 No Child Left Behind act.

Interplay of nature and nurture

Early childhood development and learning are the outcome of the interactions between biological influences and environmental experiences. These interactions are ongoing and dynamic in nature. For example, a child may be genetically predisposed for strong, healthy development, but environmental deprivation such as malnutrition in early childhood can impede fulfillment of that biological potential. On the other hand, a child may be diagnosed with an organic condition known to have adverse influences on development and learning; however, systematically applying interventions individualized for that child can mitigate such effects and promote the optimal possible outcomes. Also, children's interactions with adults and other children, and vice versa, reciprocally influence and are influenced by children's basic temperaments, such as extraversion or introversion. Because of the strength of the influences of both biological and experiential factors and their interactions, early childhood teachers need to hold and communicate high expectations for each child and to access their own funds of knowledge, persistence, and creativity in seeking different methods that enable each individual child's success.

Social and cultural contexts of early childhood learning

Growing children are strongly affected by multiple, interacting social and cultural contexts, including their families, educational settings, communities, and the larger society. The latter's biases, for example, sexism, racism, and related discrimination and negative stereotypes, influence all children, including those with supportive, loving families living in healthy, solid communities. Although cultural aspects in education are frequently represented as considerations for diverse, minority, and immigrant children and families, every individual is a member of, and thus influenced by, a culture. Each culture individually and characteristically organizes and views child development and behavior. Therefore, early childhood teachers must comprehend how family and sociocultural settings influence children's developing abilities and learning and recognize children's resulting varied expressions of their developmental accomplishments. Educators' sensitivity to their own cultural experiences and how these form their viewpoints is crucial, as is considering multiple perspectives, for their decision making regarding children's development and education.

Influences of children's early experiences on their development and learning

Both positive and negative experiences children have early in life exert significant accumulating effects on their development. For example, some children's preschool social interactions promote confidence and social skills, facilitating making friends later, improving both their social competencies and academic performance. When other children do not develop basic social skills early on, peers reject or ignore them, putting them at higher risk for dropout, delinquency, or mental health issues later. Children's early neurological development is enhanced by receiving ample, varied, rich environmental stimuli, furthering formation of more neural connections, which then promote additional development and learning. Children deprived of such early stimulation have less ability to develop and learn through future experiences, triggering cumulative disadvantages. The earlier the intervention and support, the more effective they are. For example, it is much easier and cheaper to prevent reading problems than remediate them. Research indicates a child's first 3 years are the optimal time for developing spoken language. Giving children necessary stimuli and supports at optimal times most consistently produces successful outcomes.

Promoting optimal emotional and social development in babies and young children

Relationships that are secure, warm, consistent, and nurturing, afforded to babies and young children by responsive adults are required for children to develop language, communication skills, emotional self-regulation, empathy, cooperation, cultural socialization, identity formation, and peer relationships. Children and adults who know one another well learn to anticipate one another's behaviors and cues. They become attuned to each other and develop trust. The attachments they form with parents and caregivers prepare them for all other relationships with children and adults. Just as trusting relationships with parents are the foundations for later interactions, positive relationships between teachers and young children also contribute to children's emotional development, social skills, and learning and achievements. Children develop high self-esteem, strong senses of self-efficacy (belief in one's ability to perform given tasks or skills), social skills for establishing connections and friendships with others, and skills for cooperation and conflict resolution through nurturing relationships with adults. Moreover, adults' positive modeling and support help children feel confident and secure in attempting new experiences and skills, furthering learning.

Globalization

As our economy becomes more global, societies also receive more multicultural influences. As they grow, young children move from learning within their families to within increasingly larger social circles and within their communities and, eventually, to learning to interact easily with others from both similar and different backgrounds. Children do have inherent capacities for learning to operate within multiple social and cultural settings and to change their uses of language and behaviors accordingly for each context. However, the realization of these capacities is a complex process. It happens gradually rather than quickly; children do not develop these abilities independently but need support from adults. Many educational experts believe that children should acquire languages and cultures in addition to native ones rather than in place of them. For example, while some advocate replacing immigrant children's native languages with English in America, these experts point out the importance of continuing fluency in native family and community languages while additionally gaining English proficiency. The same applies to native English-speaking children when acquiring new languages.

Play

Playing has been observed in all young humans and animals. Various types of play are beneficial for physical, cognitive, emotional, and social development and learning in all species. Human children develop their physical abilities and their appreciation of the outdoors and nature, practice developing skills, make sense of their environments, express their emotions and control them, interact socially with others, and develop their abilities to represent reality symbolically and to solve problems. Researchers find correlations between playing and basic abilities including self-regulation, memory, spoken language, social skills, and school success. Play includes physical play, playing with objects, pretend and dramatic play, constructive play, and playing games involving rules. From birth, children act upon their environments for the enjoyment of observing cause and effect; for example, repeatedly tossing a bottle out of the crib. Children who have had experiences observing others' make-believe behaviors will begin imitating these around age 2, for example, pretending to drink from a seashell.

By the time they are 3 to 5 years old, children expand rudimentary make-believe, representing objects with other objects, to more developed play involving planning plots, acting out roles, and interacting in these roles. As play is highly motivating, children adhere to their roles and scenario or game rules, helping them develop self-regulation and impulse control. Dramatic play also develops children's skills in planning, cooperating, and coordinating actions with others. Research finds this play cognitively, emotionally, and socially beneficial to children. One educational trend counter to these benefits is more overt adult direction in using media and activities in general: Researchers observe that children's richly imaginative, socially interactive play consequently appears to be decreasing. Adults must actively support children's early imaginative play to establish bases for later, more mature dramatic play promoting overall development. They should also use established methods for encouraging children's sustained involvement in higher-level play. Playing does not interfere with academic achievement; rather, it is found to support the requisite abilities for scholastic learning and success.

Getting to know each individual child and his or her family

By establishing personal, positive relationships with each child and his or her family, ECE teachers gain better appreciations of the child's specific needs, abilities, and interests and his or her family's child-rearing practices, goals, expectations, and values. Teachers should use what they learn from conversations with each child and family—using community translators or interpreters as needed for other languages, including sign language—to inform their planning and actions. To monitor and further young children's progress, teachers should be using a variety of methods for collecting information about each child's development and learning on an ongoing basis. ECE teachers should also be vigilant in watching for any signs in any individual child of excessive stress, or of traumatic events taking place in any child's life. When they are aware of these signs, teachers can often learn more about the events or situations they signify. They can then utilize strategies designed to relieve and minimize stress and to support young children in developing resilient responses to environmental challenges.

Establishing mutual relationships with young children's families

ECE teachers must know not only general principles of early childhood development and specific characteristics of their individual students; they must also know children's living contexts. The younger the children, the more teachers must obtain this knowledge through relationships they develop with children's families. Reciprocal relationships require cooperation, shared responsibility, mutual respect, and negotiation of any conflicts—all for achieving goals for children shared by teachers and families. Teachers create and sustain frequent, regular, bilateral communication with families for collaborative partnerships. This includes nonnative English-speaking families: Teachers use the child's home language if able or recruit volunteer translators. Families should participate in the programs' decisions about their children's caregiving and instruction. Families must be welcome in programs and be offered multiple opportunities to participate. Teachers recognize, respect, and respond to family goals and choices for children while maintaining responsibility for practices supporting children's development and learning.

Relationships between practitioners and parents and families

ECE teachers and the families of the children they teach should be mutually sharing with one another their knowledge about the individual child and also sharing their respective understandings of child development and learning. They should do this sharing as a part of their daily communications, as well as during planned conferences and meetings. ECE teachers should also support the children's families in whichever ways they find are best for enhancing the families' abilities and proficiency in making decisions for the child and family. Before a child enters an ECE program, the program's practitioners should engage the child's family as an important source of information about the child and should involve them in educational planning for their child. Once the child is enrolled in the program, program practitioners should also continue to engage the family in planning and progress assessment as an ongoing practice. ECE programs and practitioners should additionally provide children's families with connections to a range of services according to family concerns, needs, priorities, and identified resources.

Dr. Murray Bowen's family systems theory

Psychiatrist Bowen took knowledge about the human species as the result of evolution and knowledge from research into families and integrated these 2 areas through the application of systems theory. A central assumption of Bowen's theory is that human relationship systems are regulated by an emotional system that developed over billions of years of evolution. While humans use language, have higher-order thinking processes, and have a psychology and culture that are complex, they nevertheless perform all the same functions that other life forms do. Family systems theory holds that most of human behavior is influenced by the emotional system and that this emotional system is the main impetus that causes clinical problems to develop. Dr. Bowen maintains that new and more efficacious choices for solving problems within a person's family, social, and work systems can be discovered through attaining knowledge of how the emotional system functions in each of these domains. Bowen sees the family as an emotional unit, describing family interactions in terms of systems.

According to Bowen's family systems theory, families by nature involve intense emotional connections among their members. Though some people feel distance or disaffection from family members, this is found to be more subjective than objective. In reality, family members have such profound impacts upon one another's feelings, thoughts, and actions that they may be said to live within the same *emotional skin*. They react to one another's expectations, needs, and distress and recruit one another's attention, support, and approval. The reactive and interconnected nature of families causes their members' functioning to be interdependent. When one member's functioning changes, the other members' functioning ensues reciprocally. While individual families vary in their degrees of interdependence, this dynamic always exists to some extent. Bowen assumes that emotional interdependency evolved to support familial cooperation and cohesion, which are necessary for sheltering, feeding, and protecting family members.

Bowen proposed that, because families must stick together and cooperate to nurture and protect their members, families' characteristic emotional interdependence probably evolved to reinforce family unification and teamwork. However, he also found that, when tension within a family increases, it can intensify emotional interdependence processes, resulting in problems. Due to emotional connection, anxiety in 1 or more family members becomes infectious, spreading to other members. This makes their emotional interconnectedness less comforting and more stressful. Eventually, 1 or more family members feel isolated, out of control, or overwhelmed. Those who develop these negative feelings are the same members who make the most accommodations in efforts to reduce the tension of other members. Like all family systems processes, this involves mutual interactions. For instance, if some family members have unrealistic expectations of another member, the latter reacts by taking excessive responsibility or blame for their distress. Members who accommodate the most "absorb" the family's anxiety and, hence, are those most at risk for depression, physical illness, substance abuse, or infidelity.

Triangles
Triangles or 3-person relationship systems are the smallest stable systems and hence *molecules,* building blocks of larger systems. Two-person systems, or dyads, are unstable, withstanding less tension before requiring third persons. Because tension can shift among 3 relationships, triangles tolerate more tension. Despite greater stability, triangles also generate 1 odd person out, increasing tension. Excessive tension for 1 triangle spreads to a series of interconnected triangles. Behaviors in triangles indicate individuals' attempts to preserve emotional attachments to significant others, their responses to excessive intensity in attachments, and their taking sides in others' conflicts. There are always 2 insiders excluding 1 outsider trying to become an insider with 1 of them, with individual roles alternating when whoever is most uncomfortable maneuvers for change. With moderate tension, usually 1 side has conflict and 2 have harmony. With high tension, if 2 insiders conflict, 1 replaces the current outsider to let him or her fight with the other instead, seeking to regain insider status once conflict and tension abate. Two parents' intense focus on a child's problem(s) can cause the child's rebellion, depression, or illness.

Differentiation of self
Social groups, including families, influence their members' feelings, thoughts, and actions. However, the amount of pressure to conform varies among groups, and individuals' vulnerability to group pressures varies. These variations reflect different levels in differentiation of self. When an individual's sense of self is less developed, others influence his or her behavior more, and he or she tries more—actively or passively—to control

others' behavior. Bowen believes the basic raw materials of self are innate, but family relationships influence how much sense of differentiated self an individual develops. Those with poorly differentiated selves may become chameleons, agreeing with others to please them, or bullies, pressuring others to agree with them. Either form is equally threatened by disagreement. Extreme rebels disagree, but habitually or indiscriminately, and are also poorly differentiated. Those with well-differentiated selves realistically acknowledge dependence on others but can be objective during conflict, rejection, or criticism, separating fact from emotion. They can agree or disagree, resisting pressure, retaining independent thought, and being neither wimpy nor pushy. What they decide, say, and do are consistent.

Ramifications of having greater or lesser differentiation of self for families and other social groups

People with good differentiation of self recognize their realistic dependence on others but can independently make decisions important to family and society based on careful thought and principles they have developed rather than on momentary emotional reactions. They can support or reject others' viewpoints objectively, without subjective extremes of unquestioning allegiance or enmity. People with poorer differentiation of self either try to please by agreeing with others, or bully others to agree with them, or try to simulate a self through extreme rebellion but rebel against everybody or everything routinely rather than based on personal principles or individual choices. Differentiation of self exists in humans to all varying extents within the range between strong and weak differentiation. Hence, the intensity of emotional interdependence in families and other social groups varies according to its members' levels of differentiation of self. More intensely interdependent groups are less able to adapt to stressful occurrences without exacerbating chronic anxiety. This causes them to develop greater proportions of the most severe problems in society.

Nuclear family emotional system

According to Bowen, clinical symptoms and problems develop during times of protracted, increased family tension. Stressors, family adaptations to stress, and family connections with social networks or extended family determine tension levels. The nuclear family emotional system comprises 4 basic relationship patterns determining where family problems appear according to which patterns are most active. Greater tension likely increases symptom severity and produces symptoms in several members. The patterns are: (1) marital conflict—both spouses externalize their anxiety to the marriage, and each focuses on the other's faults, tries to control the other, and resists the other's attempts at control; (2) dysfunction in 1 spouse—one spouse pressures the other, who yields, and escalating tension exacerbates the subordinate spouse's anxiety; (3) impairment of 1 or more children—parents externalize anxieties on the child or children, worrying overly, and the more they focus on the child, the more the child reciprocally focuses on them, overreacting to parental expectations, needs, and attitudes, which undermines the child's differentiation from family; (4) emotional distance—consistently associated with #1 through #3, members withdraw emotionally to reduce relationship intensity, risking isolation.

Family projection process

The main way that parents pass their emotional problems to their child or children is described in Bowen's family systems theory by the family projection process, which can impair children's functioning and raise their risk for clinical symptoms. Problems from parents affecting children's lives most are relationship sensitivities, for example, blaming self or others, difficulties with others' expectations, excessive need for attention and approval, feeling responsible for others' happiness, feeling others are responsible for their own happiness and not tolerating anxiety, and acting not thoughtfully but impulsively to relieve momentary anxiety. Relatively intense projection processes cause children to develop relationship sensitivities stronger than those of their parents. These sensitivities promote behaviors that exacerbate chronic anxiety in relationship systems, increasing susceptibility to clinical symptoms. The intensity of the family projection process is related to the degree of a parent's emotional involvement with a child but not to the amount of time a parent spends with a child.

Bowen's family projection process, whereby parents transmit their problems to children, proceeds in 3 steps:
1. The parent focuses on a child because of fear that something is wrong with the child.
2. The parent construes the child's behavior as a confirmation of the parental fear.
3. The parent then treats the child as though he or she really has something wrong.

These steps are also described as *scanning, diagnosing,* and *treating.* They start early in a child's life and are perpetuated. The child's development and behavior are influenced by parental perceptions and fears, so the child eventually embodies these. The projection process becomes a self-fulfilling prophecy: Parents try to "fix" problems they believe the child has. For example, if parents see their child as having low self-esteem, they constantly try to give affirmations; the child becomes dependent on parental affirmations for self-esteem. While parents frequently feel they have slighted the child with problems, they actually devote more time and energy to worrying about that child than siblings.

The family projection process depicts how parents pass on their emotional imbalances to their children. By worrying something is wrong with a child and trying to correct it, parents unwittingly cause the child to reflect parental fears and perceptions in his or her behavior. For example, if parents worry a child lacks confidence and continually try to encourage him or her, the child comes to depend on parental encouragement—an external factor—for confidence, instead of developing it internally. Siblings less embroiled in this process have more realistic and mature relationships with parents; they develop into less reactive, needy, more goal-directed individuals. Mothers, as primary caretakers, are usually more likely to become overly emotionally involved with 1 or more children. In terms of Bowen's triangles, fathers usually are on the outside, with mother and the targeted child (or children) on the inside. These positions shift during times when the mother-child relationship experiences increased tension. Both parents are unsure relative to the child; however, typically 1 parent feigns sureness with the other's complicity.

Multigenerational transmission
Multigenerational transmission is the process whereby small variations between parents and children in differentiation of self accumulate over time to larger variations among family generations. Through relationships, information causing variations is transferred across generations. This transfer is both consciously taught and learned and unconsciously, automatically programmed through emotional responses and behaviors. Through genetics, relationships, and their interactions, information forms the individual self. While differentiation levels are similar in parents and children due to human children's long dependency duration, at least 1 sibling often develops somewhat more self-differentiation and 1 less than others because of the relationship patterns inherent in nuclear family emotional systems. Grown children choose mates with self-differentiation levels matching theirs; one of their children will be more or less self-differentiated than they are and grow

- 76 -

up to marry someone with similar self-differentiation. As this process repeats, successive generations show greater disparity. This explains greater variation within multigenerational families in marital stability, reproduction, health, longevity, education, and occupational outcomes: Relative differentiation of self influences all these.

High versus low levels of differentiation of self

Through the multigenerational transmission process, some children develop slightly higher or lower levels of differentiation of self than their parents and marry spouses with levels similar to theirs; some of their children do likewise; eventually, these differences become magnified over generations. Thus, small differences between parents and children become more marked differences among a family's multiple generations. These differences affect overall life functioning, including health, life span, reproduction, marriage stability, education, and work. Individuals with high differentiation of self typically have nuclear families with great stability and make many contributions to society. Those with poor differentiation of self have disorganized personal lives and are overly dependent on others' support. Multigenerational transmission significantly implies that the origins of both the most exemplary human achievements and the most serious human difficulties go back generations. The process programs not only individuals' levels of self but also their interactions with others. An individual programmed by family for intense attachments and dependency will probably choose a spouse who also attaches intensely but is directive and controlling.

Emotional cutoff

Emotional cutoff, that is, decreasing or completely cutting off emotional contact with family members, is a way people manage unresolved family emotional issues. Some people move away and rarely visit their families; others stay there but avoid confronting sensitive matters. While cutoff may preserve an appearance of better relationships, hidden problems remain unresolved. Cutoff decreases tension in original-family interactions; however, an individual may consequently overemphasize his or her new relationships' importance, potentially pressuring his or her spouse, children, and friends to meet his or her needs or making excessive efforts to meet their expectations and to protect these relationships. New relationships normally start out smoothly, but entrenched patterns of the original family's dynamics eventually surface, creating tension. People who are emotionally cut off may attempt to bring their intimate relationships stability by turning work and social relationships into substitute "families."

Individuals form different types of attachments to their original families. Some parts of their attachments are always unresolved. Unresolved attachments can appear in many different forms, including these 3 examples:
1. An individual regresses to feeling childlike when visiting his or her parents, expecting parents to make decisions for him or her that he or she normally makes independently.
2. An individual experiences guilt when around his or her parents, feeling that he or she must solve the parents' problems, resolve their conflicts, or alleviate their distress.
3. An individual feels that his or her parents do not appear to approve of or understand him or her, and consequently has an enraged reaction.

Unresolved attachment

The real source of unresolved attachment is both the parents' and the adult child's immaturity. However, it is typical for individuals experiencing unresolved attachment to blame either themselves or other people for the problems occurring. Although everybody has some amount of unresolved attachment to his or her original family, those with higher differentiation of self have far more resolution than those with lower differentiation of self.

All grown children have unresolved attachments to their families of origin to some extent. Adult children may move away from their original families and seldom visit as a form of emotional cutoff. When they do visit, they may hope interactions will be better and look forward to this. However, according to Bowen's family systems theory, nuclear family emotional systems are characterized by certain patterns of interactions. These patterns become so habitual that individuals repeat them automatically; they are reactivated when adult children visit their original families, usually within a short time. In some families, these patterns cause interactions to devolve into obvious fighting. In others, relations seem harmonious on the surface, but strong emotions lurk just beneath. Even short visits can exhaust all members. Parents become so reactive that they are relieved when a highly emotionally cutoff adult child departs or stays away; siblings are often enraged at him or her for upsetting their parents. Families do not desire such interactions; however, all members are so sensitive that their contact cannot be comfortable.

Individual development and behavior

Neo-Freudian psychiatrist Alfred Adler first proposed that a child's birth order influenced his or her personality. Later, psychologist Walter Toman researched the position of siblings within a family and its effect on personality and behavior development. Murray Bowen incorporated Toman's findings into his family systems theory as he found them so consistent with his own thinking. They both believed that people develop similar significant traits in common with others growing up in the same sibling position. For example, oldest children tend to lead, while youngest children tend to follow. Youngest children who like being in charge typically demonstrate different leadership styles from oldest siblings. Positions are not considered better or worse but complementary: Oldest-child bosses may work best with youngest-child assistants. Toman found sibling position affects spouses' probability of divorcing. An older brother of a younger sister has less chance of divorcing when marrying another younger sister with an older brother. An older brother of a brother who marries an older sister of a sister has more chance of divorce.

Differing probabilities of divorce

Older brothers of younger sisters marrying younger sisters of older brothers are less likely to divorce than older brothers of brothers marrying older sisters of sisters. This is because, in the former situation, each spouse is used to living with the opposite sex, and each duplicates his or her rank in the original family. But in the latter, neither spouse grew up with an opposite-sex sibling, and neither married into a complementary rank position. The older brother of a brother and older sister of a sister may clash over control. Two youngest children marrying may clash over who gets to be more dependent. Differences among individuals with the same sibling positions are explained partly by differentiation of self. An oldest child who feels anxiety rather than comfort regarding leadership or responsibility may develop indecision and reactivity to expectations; the younger sibling may become the *functional oldest* in the family system. Anxiously focused youngest children may become especially helpless and demanding. Conversely, 2 more mature youngest children may have a very successful marriage.

Sibling order's influence on relationships

Toman and Bowen both found certain characteristics and variations in individuals' personalities, behaviors, and relationships according to their positions among siblings in their original families. Not only birth order but also individual sibling roles affect development. For example, sometimes the chronologically oldest sibling is uncomfortable with a leadership role, and a younger sibling assumes it, becoming the *functional oldest*. When a youngest child who is very mature marries another mature youngest child, they are at much lower risk of divorcing than couples wherein 1 or both spouses were immature youngest children. Middle children function showing characteristics of 2 sibling positions. A girl with an older brother and a younger sister typically demonstrates some characteristics of a younger sister of a brother and some of an older sister of a sister. Another significant factor is the sibling positions of an individual's parents. The oldest child of parents who were both the youngest children in their respective families meets with different parental expectations than one whose parents were both oldest children.

Societal emotional process

Bowen's theory both describes family dynamics and also applies to occupational and social nonfamily groups. The societal emotional process depicts how the influences of emotional systems on behavior extend to the level of society, causing alternately progressive and regressive eras. While cultural influences significantly affect societal functioning, they do not adequately explain these fluctuations in societal adaptations to challenges. While treating families with juvenile delinquents, Dr. Bowen discovered that society's responses to them mirrored families' responses. In trying to give delinquent children unconditional love, families tried but failed to control them. Children sensed parents' uncertainty, resisted their attempts at control, and ignored their punishments. Bowen found that, after World War II, society started regressing, worsening in the 1950s and quickly escalating in the 1960s. Societal institutions including schools, governments, and the juvenile court system, reflected parental behaviors regarding delinquents. He described this regression as driven by need to relieve existing anxiety instead of acting according to principles and long-term perspectives.

Symptoms of societal regression

According to Bowen's description of the societal emotional process, societies reflect the same interactional patterns observed within families on a larger level. Societies go through progressive and regressive periods. In progressive times, people take actions based on principles and considerations for the long-term future; in regressive times, people instead take actions reactively to alleviate their current anxieties. Symptoms of societal regression include increasing divorce rates, climbing crime and violence rates, more racial polarization, rising bankruptcy rates, drug abuse epidemics, more litigious behavior, and more attention to rights than to responsibilities, and leadership's decision making becoming less principled. Recent regressive signs appear related to factors including the population explosion, natural resource depletion, and a sense of decreasing frontiers. Bowen predicted that, as in families, societal regression continues until taking the easy way out in difficult matters results in consequences worse than those of making long-term decisions. He predicted human society living in greater harmony with nature by the mid-21st century.

Delivery of Specially Designed Instruction

Trends in early childhood education (ECE)

Before World War II, ECE made slow progress toward unification, and progress was not measured. However, after World War II, influences such as many new job opportunities for women have furthered more global unifying of ECE programs. The advent of Head Start and Early Head Start provided models for making use of the most critical time in child development and have been important parts of the unification process. Today, the majority of ECE school settings are centralized on the basis of teachers', learning assistants', and administrators' educational qualifications in the ECE field. To become ECE educators, candidates must pass tests to obtain degrees, certifications, and licensure, required by both federal and state governments. ECE learning is based on existing scientific research measures and on children's learning capacities. However, ECE teachers have varied educational backgrounds, including philosophy, mathematics, music, psychology, social sciences, literature, and the arts. Teacher requirements include a bachelor's degree from an accredited university or college, licensure or certification from a state board of education, and passing a national accreditation body's educational requirements.

In recent years, social changes have affected the ECE field. There is a shortage of quality infant and child care. More immigration has increased issues of English as a second language (ESL), home languages and cultures, and school cultures. Many more special needs children are in EC settings today. America has a shortage of well-qualified teachers. The EC field, particularly child care, is underfunded and rapidly losing well-prepared administrative and teaching personnel. Future projections are for substantially increasing demands for early child education and care, dramatically increasing cultural and linguistic diversity, and more poverty in families with young children. The largest demographic change predicted for future decades affecting young children is more ESL children in America. Another significant factor today is increased political and public awareness of the impact of the EC period upon children's futures. EC educators identify challenges including increasing all child achievement, decreasing learning gaps, improving preschool and elementary education and connecting them better, and increasing recognition of teachers' knowledge and decision making as crucial to effective education.

No Child Left Behind

NCLB created a national policy in America to make schools accountable for eradicating achievement gaps that persist among diverse child groups. The law's purpose was to assure equality in education. It requires disaggregated, separate reporting of standardized achievement test scores of English language learners, special education students, racial and ethnic minorities, and economically disadvantaged students. It also requires annual gains in achievement be made in each of these groups. The aim is to keep schools responsible for effective instruction of all students. However, much controversy surrounds whether schools can attain the intended outcomes. Also, criticisms include that accountability legislation has unintentional, undesirable effects like restricting curriculum, excessive testing, and inappropriate testing methods. Although the public may not support the accountability movement's methods, the majority does support its goals for uniformly high achievement. Educators such as the National Association for the Education of Young Children (NAEYC) see this attitude as a demand for educators to enhance student achievement and close gaps wasting children's potential and harming their future prospects.

The movement for school accountability in educating all American children has not only affected public education beginning with kindergarten; it has also influenced preschool education. By 2007, greater than ¾ of U.S. states had established early learning standards, and the other ¼ were developing these. The Head Start program has established a child outcomes framework that defines educational expectations in 8 domains of learning. U.S. public policy statements and national reports espouse widespread efforts to improve early childhood teaching and learning for the purpose of developing greater school readiness; these efforts include creating standards-based curricula and assessment for early childhood learning. The issues of enabling all children's success and eliminating learning gaps are not new but are receiving more attention in the current context of accountability. Emerging scientific evidence and innovative teaching practices are being used to guide the ECE field regarding what skills and knowledge teachers must particularly cultivate in young children and how they can do this.

Separation between preschool and elementary education

America's preschool and elementary education have long been separate in their infrastructures, traditions, values, and funding sources. The American educational establishment has not viewed preschool as a complete component of public education, largely because preschool is not required and often not publicly funded. Additionally, the sponsorship, delivery systems, and teacher credentials in preschool programs vary widely. Many such programs began to provide child care for working parents. However, recently the educational potentials and aims of preschools have gained more recognition. This awareness adds to a softening of boundaries between preschool and elementary education. Educators now call for increased collaboration and continuity between the two. Accountability laws mandating third-grade standardized testing put greater pressure on K–2 teachers, who then rely on preschool educators to prepare children for K–2. Also contributing is an increase in state-funded prekindergarten, now serving more than a million 3- and 4-year-olds; additional millions are in child care and Head Start programs meeting state pre-K requirements and receiving state pre-K funding.

Government funding for and attendance in preschool and kindergarten

Head Start now serves more than 900,000 children nationally and is required at the state level to coordinate with public school systems. At least 300,000 children receive preschool education and services funded by Title I monies. Approximately 35% of 4-year-olds in America are in publicly funded prekindergarten programs. Because there are not enough affordable yet high-quality programs for children below age 5, and workers in such programs typically receive low pay, proponents expect advantages from having public funding provide educational services to more 4-year-olds and possibly even 3-year-olds. Advocates also see an advantage of better connection between preschool and elementary education programs in that they can learn from each other, affording more continuity and congruence from pre-K through grade 3. Disadvantages anticipated by preschool educators include excessive influence on early childhood by public K–12 schools pressured for accountability by high-stakes testing. Already seeing adverse effects on K–3 students, educators fear these extending to younger children. Early childhood education generally supports early learning standards in principle but in practice may doubt their adverse consequences.

Aligning preschool and elementary educational standards

Educators find preschool-elementary standards alignment crucial for their effectiveness. Some note that what they call *downward mapping,* that is, taking standards for older children and simplifying them for younger children, is not realistic and hence not effective. They recommend that early learning standards should be developed on the bases of research-based and practice-based evidence about children from diverse backgrounds at specific ages and developmental stages and about sequences, processes, variations, and long-term outcomes of early development and learning. Currently, though educators are discussing the establishment of a framework for national standards, this does not yet exist, and individual state standards vary without alignment. Accordingly, textbook and curriculum publishers striving to be competitive in the market attempt to address all state standards. Teachers, feeling pressure to cover these myriad topics, touch only fleetingly and shallowly upon each. This sacrifices in-depth knowledge and concentration on and mastery of fewer, more central learning goals.

Teachers' roles as decision makers in early childhood education

Accountability and standards have caused U.S. states and education stakeholders to define what knowledge and abilities children should have at respective grade levels and demand rapid progress in achievement across all student groups. Therefore, many administrators and policy makers prefer strategies and tools meant to expedite these results, including curricula, lessons, and schedules that are "teacher-proofed." In some state and district publicly-funded early childhood (EC) settings, teachers report much less freedom than before, or none, to decide on curricula, assessments, or even how they use class time. The question emerges regarding the balance between how much teacher independence is optimal for child learning and how much direction and support of teachers' practices furthers this end. Many school administrators lack early childhood education (ECE) backgrounds and cannot judge best EC practices. ECE teachers have this specialized knowledge and daily classroom interaction with children. However, due to no standards for entry-level ECE credentials, diverse program settings and conditions, low pay, and high turnover, many EC teachers also lack current preparation in some parts of the curriculum.

Early learning standards in the United States

The Good Start, Grow Smart legislation passed in 2002 mandated early learning standards for language, literacy, and mathematics, so such standards are fairly recent. Some U.S. states have applied these standards comprehensively across developmental and learning domains; others concentrate mainly on the legally mandated areas, especially literacy. When a state does not develop comprehensive standards, the ensuing curriculum will also be less comprehensive. Any alignment between preschool and elementary education would probably be restricted to those few curriculum elements named by the standards. In addition to narrowing the scope of curriculum, many state standards overestimate or underestimate young children's abilities by adhering to shallow learning objectives rather than addressing desired child abilities and knowledge and aligning with age and grade, developmental levels, developmental sequences, and learning characteristics. Predominantly English-language assessments are also of concern because they prohibit

- 82 -

demonstration of significant knowledge by English-as-a-second-language (ESL_ English-language-learner (ELL) students.

Standards overload

Because current learning standards vary among U.S. states with no nationalized standards, publishers of curriculum materials try to address all state standards, resulting in too many standards that teachers feel they must cover. This becomes overwhelming to both teachers and children. Additional adverse effects upon preschool, kindergarten, and first-grade teaching practices include too much whole-class and group lecturing, teaching separate objectives in a fragmented or unconnected manner, and forcing teachers to adhere to rigid schedules with tight paces. Another result is that, in these practices, schools sacrifice important experiences for children in problem solving, peer collaboration, emotional and social development, physical and outdoor activities, arts activities, and rich play activities. Professional educators are concerned that high-pressure teaching environments prevent children from developing senses of self-efficacy, competence, choice-making ability, love of learning, and the expansiveness and joy of childhood learning. Many educators aver that preschool-primary collaboration is not meant to teach elementary school skills earlier but to assure that younger children develop optimally and learn the basic skills they will need for future school learning.

Limited autonomy in early childhood education (ECE) settings

Due to the complexity of learning and teaching processes, all of a teacher's decisions and actions cannot be directed in advance. When programs or administrators gravitate toward practices expediting accountability pressures and standards, teachers lose autonomy to decide on curriculum, assessments, and even disposition of classroom time. Good teachers must be allowed to apply their knowledge, expertise, and judgment to decisions benefiting their students. However, autonomy does not dictate isolation: Teachers must also be given supports, tools, and resources to make solid instructional choices. A school or program's proven curriculum framework is a good basis for guiding curriculum development. Teachers can then apply their skills and experience in adapting curriculum optimally for their students. Teachers should be given professional development associated with curriculum frameworks and collaborative opportunities. Curricular direction helps teachers choose effective learning strategies, experiences, and materials to meet learning goals. Not having to create entire curricula, they can concentrate on instructional decisions. Many ECE personnel are insufficiently prepared; addressing this is informed by recent research into critical teaching factors.

Inform best practices in the field of early childhood education (ECE)

Recent research findings show hope for decreasing learning barriers and gaps and increasing all children's performance. More knowledge has been discovered regarding which competencies in physical, cognitive, emotional, social, and academic areas enable young children's meeting their full potentials for development and learning. These findings help decide curriculum sequences and content for all children but particularly to help children entering school with lower basic skills levels, including children of poverty, children of color, and English language learners. Research is also helping EC educators to assure early intervention for children with learning disabilities. Research confirms the superior effectiveness of earlier, sometimes intensive, intervention over reactive or remedial (too little, too late) approaches. For instance, the comprehensive, 2-generation Early Head Start program for children up to age 3 and their families has been proven by research to enhance cognitive, linguistic, emotional, and social development. While such high-quality infant and toddler services in America are scarce, they produce enduring positive effects on child development, learning, and emotional self-regulation.

Promoting preliteracy skills

Research finds that young children's vocabulary knowledge and other spoken language elements significantly predict their later reading comprehension. Although young children with limited vocabularies may learn basic decoding skills, they are nonetheless likely to have problems by grade 3 or 4, when they must read about different subjects in more advanced texts. Deficient comprehension caused by deficient vocabulary inhibits success across the curriculum. This difficulty is compounded for students hearing little or no English at home. Early childhood education (ECE) programs beginning proactive vocabulary development early can mitigate achievement gaps for these students. EC teachers should engage children in linguistic interactions throughout their days. For example, they can read to small groups of children and then engage them in discussions about the stories. Recent research has discovered that extended discourse, that is, conversations between children and adults on any given topic, continued across multiple sessions or instances, is particularly beneficial to young children's language development.

Recent research has found strong evidence that phonological awareness, alphabetic knowledge, and print awareness in young children significantly predict their reading and writing proficiency when they are older. About 10 to 15 years ago, many teachers of preschoolers did not view teaching preliteracy skills as being a part of their jobs or even as being appropriate. Because of more recent research findings, though, it has become apparent that giving young children familiarity and practice with recognizing, differentiating, breaking down, and combining speech sounds, with the letters of the alphabet and their correspondence to and symbolic representation of speech sounds and with printed texts and how they are used, are important prekindergarten foundations for later literacy. Though many early childhood classrooms still need considerable improvements in their treatment of early literacy, at least the profession of ECE now realizes that providing such literacy foundations is an important aspect of preschool children's learning experience.

Teaching numeracy skills

Typically, prekindergarten teaching currently addresses math very little. One reason for this oversight is that ECE teachers are frequently missing preparation, skills, and self-confidence to give more attention to math in their curriculums. This omission is not trivial: Research has found that preschool children's knowledge of numbers and numerical sequences strongly predicts their mathematics success in higher grades. Not only does early numeracy predict success in later math learning; moreover, it also predicts success in later student literacy. Educational professionals and researchers find the curriculum and teaching practices used in ECE will require substantial strengthening to incorporate sufficient numeracy (and literacy) concepts. They observe that methods exist to teach young children foundational numeracy and literacy skills in developmentally appropriate and engaging ways but have not yet been included in most ECE programs. Doing so would improve children's school readiness and achievement, reduce achievement gaps within the U.S.

population, and improve overall U.S. student performance relative to that of other developed nations.

Promoting and predicting academic success

Professionals have known for some time that good emotional, behavioral, and social adjustment in young children—at home, in educational settings, and throughout life—is valuable for its own sake. However, in recent years, research studies have established that a number of emotional, social, and behavioral factors are also associated with better cognitive skills and school achievement. For example, how well children transition to formal schooling and how well they do in elementary grades are predicted by variables like self-regulation, cooperation, independence, and responsibility. The early childhood education (ECE) field has long designated emotional self-regulation a primary developmental goal for young children. Recent research findings support this by showing that young children's self-regulation skills are predictive of their later skills in focused attention, planning, problem solving, decision making, and metacognition (i.e., thinking about thinking or understanding one's own cognitive processes and using that understanding to select and apply effective learning strategies). These contribute to learning success. Additionally, children from adverse life situations, when helped to develop strong self-regulation, are better prepared for school success.

Promoting ECE elementary continuity

Researchers have investigated a number of ECE practices that predict children's success. These include strong curriculum content; teachers adhering carefully to established learning sequences in literacy, math, sciences, physical education, and so on; and focusing on developing children's emotional self-regulation, focused attention, and engagement in learning. Some additional practices that are familiar specifically to educators in the ECE field that afford positive outcomes for young children include relationship-based learning and teaching; establishing partnerships with children's families; adapting instruction for children from diverse linguistic, cultural, ethnic, religious, and socioeconomic backgrounds; individualizing instruction for specific children; providing children with active learning experiences; making learning activities meaningful to children; and having classes with smaller sizes. Educational researchers recommend extending these beneficial practices to elementary grades on a widespread basis. Also, some recent pilot projects emerging nationwide involve schools encompassing pre-K through grade 3, exploring ways to enhance alignment, continuity, and cohesion. Researchers are studying some of these programs to learn more about connecting EC and elementary education.

Areas of knowledge that early childhood education (ECE) teachers should consider to make decisions in their work with young children in all of its aspects

ECE teachers should consider the areas of knowledge about: (1) child development and learning, (2) each individual child, and (3) cultural and social contexts in which children live.
1. Teachers' knowledge of child development and learning enables them to predict generally what children typically can and cannot do at specific ages, how they behave, and optimal teaching approaches and strategies and to know individual children in an age or developmental group are always the same in some ways but

differ in others. This knowledge informs decisions regarding materials, environments, activities, and interactions.

2. Knowing each child as an individual allows teachers to address diagnosed and undiagnosed special learning needs; learning styles; personalities; strengths, interests, and preferences; prior experience and knowledge; background and living circumstances; and variations across contexts, domains, disciplines, and time.

3. Knowing children's cultural and social contexts helps teachers understand what makes sense to them; how they use language, show respect, and interact with friends versus new acquaintances; and rules for dressing, personal space, time, and so on, informing how teachers shape children's learning environments.

Principles related to developmentally appropriate practice

1. One general principle in ECE is that all domains, for example, physical, cognitive, emotional, or social, are significant and are closely interrelated. Child development in one domain influences and is influenced by development and influences in other domains. For example, motor development in infants and toddlers affords greater environmental exploration; hence, motor development influences their cognitive development and psychosocial development of a sense of autonomy. Language development affects young children's ability to engage in social interactions; ensuing social experiences further influence additional language development, showing the reciprocal interrelation of linguistic and social development.

2. Another principle is that many areas of child growth and development follow a fairly predictable, stable order; more advanced skills and knowledge build upon those attained earlier. For example, learning to count is a foundation for later understanding numbers and then learning math. While many changes are predictable, the ways they manifest and their associated meanings can vary greatly across various cultural and linguistic contexts. Knowing developmental sequences informs practices in curriculum development and teaching.

Design of curriculum, learning environments, learning experiences, and teaching interactions

Individual children develop and learn at individually diverse rates; and different domains of individual development vary within the individual child. Patterns and schedules vary to some extent around norms; and each child is unique. Contributing variables include individual child temperaments, personalities, aptitudes and abilities, and how their experiences are influenced by familial, social, and cultural contexts. While chronological age indicates general developmental levels, within these, each child can differ greatly. Teachers often must deploy added resources and actions to assure optimal learning and development in children with special abilities or needs and when children's background experiences do not prepare them for certain educational settings. Thus, teachers should individualize curricular, teaching, and interactional decisions insofar as they can. Inflexibly expecting performance based on group norms does not account for knowledge of true developmental and learning variations. Nonetheless, teachers must maintain high expectations of all children and must supply resources and utilize methods to aid them in fulfilling those expectations.

Children's approaches to learning

National experts on educational goals and planning identify approaches to learning as included among several aspects of children's school readiness. Approaches to learning emphasize not the what of learning but the how. They include children's feelings related to learning, for example, motivation, interest, and pleasure in learning; and children's behaviors during learning, for example, attention, flexibility, persistence, and self-regulation. Even the youngest children vary in approaches to learning, which can affect school readiness and achievement. Research studies find children more eager to learn upon beginning school have more success in reading and math than children less motivated. Children exhibiting more positive learning-related behaviors like attention, initiative, and persistence develop better language skills later. Kindergarteners showing such skills plus better self-regulation demonstrate greater reading and math skills in higher grades. While temperament and other individual differences influence approaches to learning, early family and educational experiences also exert strong effects. Research supports the effectiveness of working with families; strengthening relationships with children; and choosing appropriate and effective methods of curriculum, assessment, and instruction.

Accountability of all members of the learning community to promote all members' learning and well-being

It takes time and experience for young children to develop self-regulation and responsibility for themselves and toward others. Teachers realizing this can plan their curriculums and interactions with children toward furthering such development. In addition to teaching pro-social behaviors, teachers are also responsible for observing behaviors that impede learning or disrespect the learning community and for anticipating, preventing, and redirecting such behaviors. Effective teachers establish and consistently apply clear, reasonable limits for children's behavior. They assist children in being accountable to themselves and others for their behaviors. They may even involve preschoolers in developing their own behavioral rules for the learning community. Teachers must hear and acknowledge children's emotions, including frustration; respectfully respond in ways understandable to young children; supply guidance in conflict resolution; and model problem-solving skills. Good teachers should also model superior levels of self-regulation and responsibility for young children through their own interactions with other adults and children.

Controlling physical and psychological conditions in the learning environment

ECE practitioners can protect learning children's health and safety by supporting their physical needs for sensory stimulation, physical activity, rest, nourishment, and fresh air and outdoor activity. They can balance children's daily schedules between physical activity and rest and give them opportunities to interact with nature. Psychologically, ECE practitioners should make children feel safe, secure, comfortable, and relaxed in their learning experiences and interactions with other learning community members rather than causing feelings of fear, worry, disengagement, or excessive stress. ECE teachers should promote children's interest and enjoyment in learning. By organizing the environment and creating orderly schedules and routines, ECE teachers give young children stability and structure that are conducive to learning. Dynamically varying aspects of the environment provide variety, while such teacher-created stability and structure still maintain the overall learning situation's comprehensibility and predictability from young children's perspectives. ECE teachers can additionally maintain optimally positive psychological, emotional, and social learning climates by assuring that children's home languages and cultures are represented in their classrooms' daily activities and interactions.

Scaffolding relative to early childhood education (ECE)

Scaffolding is support that adults lend to youngsters while they learn a skill they have not yet mastered—just enough to enable them to perform it and gradually withdrawn as they gain proficiency until they can do it independently. Three general principles related to scaffolding are: (1) teachers realize that any single child's scaffolding needs vary through time and that skills and hence support needs vary among children and respond accordingly; (2) scaffolding can have varied forms, for example, modeling a skill, providing a cue, giving a hint, or modifying or adapting activities and materials; scaffolding can be given in varied settings, for example, planned learning activities, outdoor activities, play situations, and daily routines; (3) teachers can model a skill to provide scaffolding directly, or the teacher can plan for peers, such as learning buddies, to model it.

Appropriate curriculum planning relative to clarifying and targeting important developmental and learning goals

ECE teachers must know and clearly express their young students' developmental and learning goals. They take into account what young children should understand, know, and be able to do in the physical, cognitive, emotional, and social domains of development and the preparation and readiness they need for future learning and performance across the school disciplines in elementary and higher grades. ECE teachers should familiarize themselves thoroughly with any state mandates or standards that exist for their schools or programs. They should also provide additional goals not sufficiently addressed by these standards. In addition, regardless of where learning goals may have originated, both teachers and administrators in ECE make sure that they clearly define these goals and communicate them to young students' families and other stakeholders in the children's education and that all stakeholders understand these goals and their definitions.

Applying and adapting curriculum framework in planning their teaching

1. ECE teachers should know the key skills and comprehensions for a given child age group in the physical, cognitive, emotional, and social domains of development, including how development and learning in each domain interacts with and influences the others.
2. ECE teachers combine the curriculum framework provided to them with their own knowledge, gained through observations and other assessments, of their young students' individual language proficiencies, learning needs, progress, and interests. Teachers use care in adapting and shaping the learning experiences they offer to enable every child to attain the curriculum's goals.
3. ECE teachers use their knowledge of typical developmental sequences and paths to arrange the pace and sequence of the learning activities they provide. For children who have not had some of the previous learning opportunities that engender successful school performance, teachers adapt their curriculums in ways that will assist them to make faster progress.

Emphasizing meaningful connections among learning experiences, with child interests, and within and across learning domains

All students learn best when they are given concepts, language, and skills that relate to something familiar and important to them. This includes young children. Not only is learning facilitated through connections with prior knowledge and interests; it is also facilitated through meaningful interconnections among the new things learned, which give them more coherence.

1. ECE teachers' curriculum planning integrates children's learning, both within each of the domains—physical, cognitive, emotional, and social—and also across them. They do the same regarding readiness for school disciplines.
2. ECE teachers use children's individual interests in curriculum planning and promoting motivation and attention. Teachers also introduce children to new experiences and topics they are likely to be interested in based on their identified interests. Developing and expanding children's interests are especially important for preschoolers just learning to focus their attention.
3. ECE teachers plan logically ordered curriculum experiences that permit focusing in depth on each content area for sustained periods rather than shallowly skimming over too many areas.

Practice Test

Practice Questions

1. According to the Assistive Technology Act, assistive devices are:
   a. Electronic devices that support learning such as computers, calculators, student responders, electronic self-teaching books and electronic reading devices.
   b. Any mechanical, electrical or electronic device that helps teachers streamline efficiency.
   c. Any device that could help a disabled student in school or life functions.
   d. Experimental, high-tech teaching tools that teachers can obtain by participating in one of 67 government funded research projects.

2. A seventh grader with mild intellectual disabilities is having considerable trouble with algebra. His stepfather is trying to help, but the more he drills the girl, the less she seems to understand. The teacher suggests:
   a. He continues drilling and enhances with pop quizzes. It may take the student longer to understand algebraic terms, expressions and equations, but with hard work she will eventually learn them.
   b. He calls a moratorium on at-home algebra work. The student is becoming less willing to work at school and the teacher is concerned she is losing confidence due to failure at home.
   c. He continues drilling but breaks the study sessions into no more than 3 five-minute periods per day.
   d. He substitutes fun activities for math drills. Incorporating algebra blocks, math games, and applications of algebra to real-life situations will make math more fun and more relevant.

3. Augmentative and Alternative Communication (AAC) devices, forearm crutches and a head pointer are assistive devices that might be used by a student with:
   a. Severe intellectual disabilities.
   b. Cerebral palsy.
   c. Tourette syndrome.
   d. Minor skeletal birth defects.

4. A four-year-old child has difficulty sorting plastic cubes, circles and triangles by color and shape, doesn't recognize patterns or groups and doesn't understand the relationship between little/big, tall/short, many/few. The child enjoys counting, but does not say the numbers in proper order nor recognize the meaning of different numbers. This child most likely:
   a. Is exhibiting signs of intellectual disabilities.
   b. Is developing within an acceptable range.
   c. Has dysgraphia.
   d. Has dyscalculia.

5. Response to Intervention (RTI) is:
    a. Parents, classroom teacher, special education teacher and other caring persons stage an intervention to express how a student's socially unacceptable behavior upsets them.
    b. An opportunity for a student to openly and freely respond to specific interventions without fear of reprimand.
    c. A strategy for diagnosing learning disabilities in which a student receives research-supported interventions to correct an academic delay. If the interventions do not result in considerable improvement, the failure to respond suggests causal learning disabilities.
    d. A formal complaint lodged by a parent or guardian in response to what they consider an intrusion by a teacher into private matters.

6. Sixth graders Alfie and Honesty ride the same bus. Honesty constantly teases Alfie. Alfie is embarrassed because he believes she is berating him. The bus driver told their teacher it was possible that Honesty is actually interested in Alfie, but doesn't express it well. The best form of conflict resolution would be for the teacher to:
    a. Take Honesty aside and explain boys don't like overly aggressive girls.
    b. Take Honesty aside and teach her less embarrassing methods of getting a boy's attention.
    c. Explain to Alfie that Honesty probably teases him because she likes him and he should take it as a compliment.
    d. Suggest to Alfie that if he is disturbed by Honesty's teasing, he have a calm, assertive conversation with her and tell her he doesn't like it and insist she stop.

7. When transitioning from one subject to another and when she becomes anxious, a student always taps her front tooth 5 times then opens and closes her eyes 11 times before leaving her desk. The child most likely has:
    a. Repetitive Disorder
    b. Obsessive Compulsive Disorder
    c. Anxiety Disorder
    d. Depression

8. By law, a child with a disability is defined as one with:
    a. Intellectual disabilities, hearing, speech, language, visual, orthopedic or other health impairments, emotional disturbance, autism, brain injury caused by trauma or specific learning disabilities and needs special education and related services.
    b. Intellectual disabilities, emotional disturbance, autism, brain injury caused by trauma or specific learning disabilities who needs special education and related services.
    c. A child who is unable to reach the same academic goals as his peers, regardless of cause, and needs special education and related services.
    d. The term "disability" is no longer used. The correct term is "other ability".

9. Which classroom environment is most likely to support a student with ADHD?

a. Students with ADHD become bored easily so a classroom with distinct areas for a multitude of activities will stimulate her. When she loses interest in one area, she can move to the next and continue learning.

b. Students with ADHD are highly aggressive and easily fall into depression. The teacher needs to provide a learning environment in which sharp objects such as scissors, tacks or sharpened pencils are eliminated. This ensures greater safety for both student and teacher.

c. Students with ADHD are highly creative. A room with brightly colored mobiles, a multitude of visual and physical textures (such as striped rugs and fuzzy pillows) and plenty of art-based games will stimulate and encourage learning.

d. Students with ADHD are extremely sensitive to distractions. A learning environment in which visual and audio distractions have been eliminated is best. Low lighting, few posters and a clean whiteboard help the student focus.

10. A resource teacher notices one of her students has made the same reading error numerous times the past few days. She decides the student wrongly believes that 'ou' is always pronounced as it is in the word *through.* She corrects this misunderstanding by showing the student word families containing words like *though, ought, ground.* This strategy is called:

a. Corrective feedback

b. Positive reinforcement

c. Consistent repetition

d. Corrective support

11. A kindergarten teacher has a new student who will not make eye contact with anyone so she doesn't appear to be listening. She often rocks back and forth and does not stop when asked or give any indication she has heard. She avoids physical contact. Sometimes the teacher must take her arm to guide her from one place to another. Occasionally the student erupts, howling in terror and fury. The most likely diagnosis is:

a. Asperger's Syndrome

b. Obsessive-Compulsive Disorder

c. Autism

d. Antisocial Psychosis

12. A special education teacher shows parents of a dyslexic child a study that examined brain scans of dyslexic and non-dyslexic readers. The study demonstrated that dyslexics use (the) _____ side(s) of their brains while non-dyslexics use (the) _____ side.

a. Both, the left.

b. Both, the right.

c. Left, right.

d. Right, left.

13. A student with _____ has a great deal of difficulty with the mechanical act of writing. She drops her pencil, cannot form legible letters and cannot decode what she has written.

a. A nonverbal learning disorder

b. Dyslexia

c. Dyspraxia

d. Dysgraphia

14. A resource room teacher has a middle school student recently diagnosed with depression. The student has been put on an antidepressant. The teacher knows the student may develop certain transitory reactions to the medication. One reaction might be:
    a. Extreme sleepiness.
    b. Increased, persistent thirst.
    c. Anxiety, coupled with an urge to verbalize a continuous inner dialogue.
    d. Inappropriate anger.

15. Reading comprehension should be evaluated:
    a. Every two months using various informal assessments. Done more than twice a year, assessments place undue stress on both student and teacher and do not indicate enough change to be worth it.
    b. With a combination of informal and formal assessments including: standardized testing, awareness of grades, systematically charted data over a period of time and teacher notes.
    c. With bi-weekly self-assessment rubrics to keep the student aware of his progress.
    d. By testing the student before reading a particular text to determine which vocabulary words he already knows and can correctly use.

16. A diabetic first grader is very pale, trembling and covered in a fine sweat. The teacher attempts to talk to the child, but the girl's response is confused and she seems highly irritable She is most likely experiencing:
    a. Diabetic hypoglycemia.
    b. Lack of sleep.
    c. Hunger.
    d. Diabetic hyperglycemia.

17. An intellectually disabled teen has been offered a job by an elderly neighbor. The neighbor wants the teen to work alongside her in the garden twice a week. They will plant seeds, transplant larger plants, weed, lay mulch, water and fertilize. Later in the season, they will cut flowers and arrange bouquets, pick produce and sell them at the neighbor's roadside stand. The neighbor, the teen's mother and special education teacher meet to discuss the proposal. The plan is:
    a. Tentatively accepted. Because the teen is excited about having a job, her mother and teacher reluctantly agree. They both know the girl is likely to lose interest quickly and caution the neighbor that if she truly needs help she may want to look elsewhere. However, no one wants to disappoint the girl and all decide the experience will be good for her.
    b. Rejected. Despite the teen's insistence she can manage these tasks, her mother and teacher believe she cannot. They fear trying will set her up for failure.
    c. Rejected. The teacher and her mother are very uncomfortable with the neighbor's offer. They suspect the elderly woman is simply lonely or may be a predator who has selected an intellectually disabled victim because such children are particularly vulnerable.
    d. Enthusiastically accepted. The adults discuss a background check and the possibility the teen might discover gardening is not for her and want to quit. However, this is most likely to happen early in her employment, giving the neighbor sufficient time to find another helper.

18. Dr. Gee reads the following sentence to a group of 5th graders: "The turquoise sky is reflected in the still lake. Fat white clouds floated on the lake's surface as though the water was really another sky. It was such a beautiful day. The students were to write the word "beautiful" in the blank. One student wrote 'pretty' instead. This suggests:
    a. The student doesn't know the meaning of the word 'beautiful'.
    b. The student is highly creative and believes he can substitute a word with a similar meaning.
    c. The student did not know how to spell 'beautiful'.
    d. The student did not hear what the teacher said. He heard 'pretty' instead of 'beautiful.'

19. Autism Spectrum Disorder is also known as:
    a. Pervasive Spectrum Disorder
    b. Asperger's Syndrome
    c. Variable Developmental Disorder
    d. Artistic Continuum Syndrome

20. A third grade boy is new to the school. His teacher has noticed he happily plays with other children, redirects his attention without upset when another child rejects his offer to play and doesn't mind playing on his own. However, the boy doesn't pay attention when academic instruction is given. He continues to speak with other children, draws, or distracts himself. The teacher reminds him repeatedly to listen and follow instruction. When he does not, she moves him to a quiet desk away from the others. When isolated, the boy puts his head on the desk and weeps uncontrollably, or stares at a fixed spot and repeats to himself, "I hate myself, I hate myself. I should be dead." During these episodes, the teacher cannot break through to the student; his disconnection seems complete. The teacher has requested a conference with his parents, but they do not speak English and have not responded to her offer of a translator. The teacher should:
    a. Establish a consistent set of expectations for the child. He needs to understand there are appropriate times for play and for learning.
    b. Isolate the boy first thing. His behavior suggests manipulation. By third grade children fully understand they are expected to pay attention when the teacher is speaking. The boy is punishing the teacher with tears and repetitive self-hate, consciously or unconsciously attempting to make the teacher feel guilty.
    c. Immediately refer him to the counselor. The boy is exhibiting serious emotional distress suggesting abuse or neglect at home or outside of school.
    d. Recognize the child's highly sensitive nature; offer comfort when he acts out self-loathing. Carefully explain why he must learn to pay attention so he will use reason instead of emotion when making future choices.

21. A student with Asperger's Syndrome is most likely to display which set of behaviors?
    a. He is confrontational, argumentative and inflexible.
    b. He is fearful, shy and highly anxious.
    c. He is socially distant, focused on certain subjects to the point of obsession and inflexible.
    d. He is flighty, tearful and exhibits repetitive, ritualized behavior.

22. A special education teacher working with a group of third graders is about to begin a unit on birds. She asks the children what they know about birds. They tell her birds fly, lay eggs and build nests. She asks the students to draw a picture of a bird family. Some children draw birds in flight; one draws a mother bird with a nest of babies; another draws an egg with the baby bird inside the egg. These pre-reading activities are useful because:
    a. They help assess prior knowledge.
    b. They establish a framework in which to integrate the new information.
    c. They create a sense of excitement and curiosity.
    d. All of the above.

23. Verbal dyspraxia is:
    a. Trouble with the physical act of writing.
    b. Refusal to speak.
    c. Misplacing letters within words.
    d. A motor skill development disorder which includes inconsistent speech errors.

24. A resource room teacher has a small group of second and third graders who are struggling with reading comprehension. A useful strategy would be to:
    a. Present a list of vocabulary words before students read a particular text.
    b. Ask students to create a play about the story.
    c. Read a story aloud. Ask students to raise their hands when they hear an unfamiliar word.
    d. Have each child keep a book of new vocabulary words. Whenever an unfamiliar word is seen or heard the student should enter the word in her personal dictionary.

25. Tourette syndrome is characterized by:
    a. Facial twitches, grunts, inappropriate words and body spasms.
    b. Inappropriate words, aggressive behavior and tearful episodes.
    c. Facial twitches, grunts, extreme shyness and refusal to make eye contact.
    d. Refusal to make eye contact, rocking, spinning of objects and ritualized behavior.

26. A second grader finds it impossible to remain in her seat. She wanders around the room, sprawls on the floor and rolls back and forth when asked to do math problems and jumps up and down when waiting in line. When the teacher tells her to sit down, she rolls her eyes in apparent disgust and looks to other students for support. When she finds a student looking back, she laughs and makes a face. The teacher has noticed when a reward is attached to good behavior; the girl is consistently able to control her actions for long periods of time. But when reprimanded without the promise of a reward, she becomes angry, tearful and pouts. This child is most likely manifesting:
    a. Tourette's Syndrome
    b. Attention Deficit Hyperactivity Disorder
    c. Lack of sufficiently developed behavior and social skills
    d. Psychosis

27. ADHD refers to:
    a. Attention Deficit Hyperactivity Disorder
    b. Anxiety/ Depression Hyperactivity Disorder
    c. Aggression-Depression Hyperactivity Disorder
    d. Atkinson, Draper and Hutchinson Disability

28. Rate, accuracy and prosody are elements of:
    a. Reading fluency
    b. Reading comprehension
    c. Math fluency
    d. Algebraic function

29. When a diabetic student goes into insulin shock, she should:
    a. Call her parents to come get her.
    b. Drink a soda or eat some hard candy.
    c. Drink a high-protein shake.
    d. Put her head on the desk and wait for the episode to pass.

30. Strategies to increase reading fluency for English Language Learners include:
    a. Tape-assisted reading.
    b. Reading aloud while students follow along in their books.
    c. Asking parents to read with the child each evening.
    d. A and B.

31. The Individuals with Disabilities Education Act (IDEA) requires that members of an IEP team include:
    a. All teachers involved with the student, the parent(s) or guardian and the student (if appropriate).
    b. The classroom teacher, a special education teacher, the parent(s) or guardian, a representative of the local education agency knowledgeable about specialized instruction, someone to interpret instructional implications, the student (if appropriate) and other people invited by the parents or the school.
    c. The classroom teacher, a special education teacher, the principal or AP and the parent(s) or guardian.
    d. All teachers involved with the student, the principal or AP, the parent(s) or guardian and the student (if appropriate).

32. At the beginning of each month, a student reads a page or two from a book he hasn't seen before. The resource teacher notes the total number of words in the section and the number of times the student leaves out or misreads a word. If the student reads with more than a 10% error rate, he is:
    a. Reading with full comprehension.
    b. Probably bored and his attention is wandering.
    c. Reading at a frustration level.
    d. Missing contextual clues.

33. A Cloze test evaluates a student's:
    a. Reading fluency
    b. Understanding of context and vocabulary
    c. Phonemic skills
    d. Ability to apply the Alphabetic Principle to previously unknown material.

34. A Kindergarten teacher is showing students the written alphabet. The teacher pronounces a phoneme and one student points to it on the alphabet chart. The teacher is presenting:
    a. Letter-sound correspondence
    b. Rote memorization
    c. Predictive Analysis
    d. Segmentation

35. A resource teacher wants to design a lesson that will help first and second graders learn sight words so all the students can read their lists. She should teach them how to:
    a. Divide sight words into syllables. Considering one syllable at a time provides a sense of control and increases confidence.
    b. Recognize word families. Organizing similar words allows patterns to emerge.
    c. Sound out the words by vocalizing each letter. Using this approach, students will be able to sound out any sight word.
    d. Memorize their lists by using techniques such as songs, mnemonic devices and other fun activities. By definition, sight words cannot be decoded but must be recognized on sight.

36. Phonological awareness activities are:
    a. Oral
    b. Visual
    c. Both A and B.
    d. Semantically based.

37. It is important to teach life skills to developmentally delayed students to prepare them for life after school. Which of the following skills sets should these students be taught?
    a. Count money, plan meals, grocery shop, recognize safety concerns.
    b. Count money, order delivery meals, dating skills, how to drive.
    c. How to drive, style and hygiene tips, social strategies, dating skills.
    d. Stock market investment, hairdressing, house painting, pet care.

38. A special education teacher has done intervention with an eighth grade student with a reading disability. The student can now successfully use tactics to understand the meanings of unfamiliar words, knows words such as *crucial, criticism* and *witness* have multiple meanings and considers what she already knows to figure out a word's meaning. These features of effective reading belong to which category?
    a. Word recognition
    b. Vocabulary
    c. Content
    d. Comprehension

39. Emergent writers understand letters represent sounds, words begin with a sound that can be written as a letter and writing is a way one person captures an idea another person will read. Emergent writers pass through the following stages:
   a. Scripting the end-sound to a word (KT=cat); leaving space between words; writing from the top left to the top right and from top to bottom of the page.
   b. Scripting the end-sound to a word (KT=cat); writing from the top left to the top right and from top to bottom of the page; separating the words from one another with a space in between.
   c. Leaving space between the initial letters that represent words; writing from the top left to the top right and from top to bottom of the page; scripting the final sound of each word and the initial sound (KT=cat).
   d. Drawing a picture beside each of the initial sounds to represent the entire word; scripting the end-sound to a word (KT=cat); scripting the interior sounds that compose the entire word (KAT=cat).

40. As defined by the Individuals with Disabilities Education Act (IDEA), Secondary Transition is a synchronized group of activities that are:
   a. Results-oriented and include post-school activities, vocational education, employment support and adult services and considers the individual's strengths, preferences and interests.
   b. Socially structured and consider the individual's strengths, preferences and interests and vocational requirements.
   c. Designed to support vocational training, results-oriented and have a strong social component.
   d. Selected by the parent(s) or guardian because the student cannot choose for himself.

41. A resource teacher can facilitate the greatest achievement in emergent writers who are scripting initial and final sounds by:
   a. Suggesting they write a book to build confidence, teach sequencing, and encourage them to deeply explore ideas.
   b. Suggesting they read their stories to other students.
   c. Inviting a reporter to write about her emergent writers.
   d. Inviting parents or guardians for a tea party at which the children will read their stories aloud.

42. At what point should the teacher in the above example offer the children picture books and ask them to read to her?
   a. When the children are able to script initial sounds, end sounds and interior sounds. She should wait until this point to avoid frustration.
   b. After the teacher has read the picture books several times, the children can 'practice reading' to her, while learning to handle books, turn pages, and pay attention to context clues.
   c. After the children have learned the sight words.
   d. From the first day of school. Picture walks help young readers understand books are arranged sequentially. Pictures provide narrative coherence and contextual clues. Holding a book and turning pages also gives young readers a familiarity with them.

43. How can a teacher teach spelling effectively?
   a. Students who have an understanding of letter-sound association do not need to be taught to spell. If they can say a word, they can spell it.
   b. Students who have an understanding of letter-sound association and can identify syllables and recognize when the base word has a Latin, Greek or Indo-European ancestry don't need to be taught to spell. They can deduce what is most likely the correct spelling using a combination of these strategies. A teacher who posts charts organizing words into their ancestor families, phonemic units and word-sound families is efficiently teaching spelling. The rest is up to the student.
   c. Students who spell poorly will be at a disadvantage for the rest of their lives. It is essential students spend at least 15 minutes a day drilling spelling words until they know them forward and backward. The teacher should alternate between students individually writing a new word 25 times and the entire class chanting the words.
   d. Students should be taught writing is a process. By applying spelling patterns found in word families, the spelling of many words can be deduced.

44. A special education teacher gives a struggling reader a story with key words missing:

   The children were hungry. They went into the _____. They found bread, peanut _____ and jelly in the cupboard. They made _____. They _ _ the sandwiches. Then they were not _____ anymore.

   The student is able to complete the sentences by paying attention to:
   a. Syntax. Word order can provide enough hints that a reader can predict what happens next.
   b. Pretext. By previewing the story, the student can determine the missing words.
   c. Context. By considering other words in the story, the student can deduce the missing words.
   d. Sequencing. By ordering the ideas, the student can determine the missing words.

45. Collaborative Strategic Reading (CSR) depends upon which two practices?
   a. Cooperative learning and reading comprehension.
   b. Reading and metacognition.
   c. Reading comprehension and metacognition.
   d. Cooperative learning and metacognition.

46. Before being assigned to a special education classroom, a student must:
   a. Agree to the reassignment.
   b. Have an Individualized Education Plan developed.
   c. Have an Independent Education Policy developed.
   d. Be seen by an educational psychologist to confirm her diagnosis.

47. When asked a question, the new student answers with as few words as possible. He prefers to draw airplanes over and over again rather than play with the other children. The classroom teacher isn't sure how to help the child. The special education teacher suggests the teacher:
    a. Leave the child alone. He is likely adjusting to the new situation and will come out of his shell soon enough.
    b. Remind other children in the class to include the new student.
    c. Observe the child over the course of a week or two. Draw him into conversation to determine if vocabulary is limited. Note how the child interacts with others in the class. Does he initiate conversation? If another child initiates, does he respond?
    d. Refer him to the school counselor immediately. It is likely the child is suffering from serious problems at home.

48. A special education teacher feels some of his strategies aren't effective. He asks a specialist to help him improve. The specialist suggests he:
    a. Begin a journal in which he considers strategies he has used. Which seemed to work? Which didn't, and why?
    b. Meet with the specialist to discuss the teacher's goals.
    c. Permit the specialist to drop into his classroom unannounced to observe. This will prevent the teacher from unconsciously over-preparing.
    d. Set up a video camera and record several student sessions to review. They can effectively collaborate at that time.

49. An eighth grade student is able to decode many words and has a borderline/acceptable vocabulary, but his reading comprehension is quite low. He can be helped with intervention offering:
    a. Strategies to increase comprehension and build vocabulary.
    b. Strategies to increase comprehension and learn to identify syntax.
    c. Strategies to improve understanding of both content and context.
    d. Strategies to develop vocabulary and improve understanding of both content and context.

50. Research indicates oral language competency in emergent readers is essential because:
    a. It enhances students' phonemic awareness and increases vocabulary.
    b. The more verbally expressive emergent readers are, the more confident they become. These students will embrace both academic and independent reading levels.
    c. Strong oral language skills invite students to consider a plethora of ideas. The more they ask, the richer their background knowledge.
    d. It demonstrates to students their ideas are important and worth sharing.

51. A teacher has shown a mentally challenged student a website that integrates music and video clips with a variety of educational games about a topic the student has shown interest in. The student is initially intimidated and fears interacting with the program might result in her breaking the computer. The teacher reassures her she cannot harm the machine and shows the girl how to manipulate the mouse and keyboard. The teacher reminds the student what she already knows about the subject. As the student becomes more comfortable with the mouse, she focuses on the images and sounds, at times responding to the program conversationally, telling it what she knows about dinosaurs. The teacher is using the computer along with which teaching strategy?
a. Modular instruction.
b. Scaffolding.
c. Linking.
d. Transmutation.

52. A student has been identified with a cluster of learning disabilities. She will be joining a special education classroom. She is understandably nervous about making the change to a different teacher and group of classmates. In order to help her make the transition, the child should:
a. Have a party to which her new classmates are invited along with some friends from the fifth-grade class she is leaving.
b. Prepare to begin classes with her new teacher the next day. Once the decision has been made, nothing will be gained by postponing the inevitable.
c. Be brave and understand life will be full of transitions. This is an opportunity to learn new skills that will serve her well in the future.
d. Visit the classroom, meet the teacher and her new classmates and be given the opportunity to ask questions about the change she is about to make.

53. A student is taking a reading test in which several words have been replaced with blanks. Below each blank is a series of three possible answers. The student chooses the right answer from each set. The student is taking:
a. A Cloze test, which is a type of Maze test.
b. A Maze test, which is a type of Cloze test.
c. A multiple-choice quiz.
d. A vocabulary test incorporating a type of multiple-choice quiz.

54. A teacher has a student with dyscalculia who has trouble organizing addition and subtraction problems on paper. She can best help him by:
a. Encouraging memorization of number families. Committing them to memory is the only way.
b. Demonstrating a problem in different ways. Write a problem on the board: 11 - 3. Gather 11 books and take 3 of them away. Draw 11 x's on the board and erase 3.
c. Use graph paper to help him organize. Show him how to write the problems, keeping each number in a box aligned with other numbers.
d. Make a game of addition and subtraction problems. Divide the class into groups and let them compete to see which group can solve the most problems.

55. A child has been losing strength in her muscles over a period of time. The loss is very gradual, but the teacher is concerned and would like the child to see a doctor. The possible diagnosis is:
    a. Cerebral Palsy
    b. Muscular Dystrophy
    c. Muscular Sclerosis
    d. Spastic Muscular and Nerve Disorder

56. A middle school student is preparing to transition from a self-contained special education classroom to a general education classroom. This transition should be made:
    a. With proper preparation. A student this age needs to acclimate socially and can best do so with the same group of students in every class.
    b. At the beginning of the next school year so the student doesn't have a stigma when joining the new group.
    c. One class at a time with the special education teacher supervising academic and social progress.
    d. By transitioning into classes he is most interested in because he is most likely to succeed with subjects he cares about. The confidence he gains from academic success will support him as he transitions into classes he's less interested in.

57. The four required activities described by the Assistive Technology Act (AT ACT) of 1998 are a public awareness program, coordinating activities among state agencies, technical assistance and training and
    a. Specialized training for special education teachers and support.
    b. Outreach to underrepresented religious groups, ethnicities and urban populations.
    c. Outreach to underrepresented and rural populations.
    d. New technologies training on a quarterly basis for special education teachers and support.

58. Behavior problems in special education students are most effectively handled with:
    a. Zero tolerance.
    b. Positive Behavioral Support (PBS)
    c. Acceptance and tolerance
    d. Positive Behavioral Control (PBC)

59. A teacher suspects one of her kindergarteners has a learning disability in math. Why would the teacher suggest intervention to the child's concerned parents rather than assessment as the first step?
    a. She wouldn't; assessment should precede intervention.
    b. She wouldn't; kindergarteners develop new skills at radically different rates. Suggesting either intervention or assessment at this point is premature. The teacher would more likely observe the child over a three month period to note her development before including the parents about her concern.
    c. Assessing a young child for learning disabilities often leads to an incorrect conclusion because a student must be taught the subject before it's possible to assess her understanding of it. Intervention teaches the child specific skills to correct her misconceptions. If the intervention fails, assessment is the next step.
d. Assessment at this stage is unnecessary and wastes time and money. Since an assessment that resulted in a diagnosis of a learning disability would recommend

60. IDEA requires that students identified with learning disabilities or other special needs be educated in _____ learning environment appropriate for their needs.
  a. The safest
  b. The least restrictive
  c. The most appropriate
  d. The most desirable

61. Howard Gardner's theory of Multiple Intelligences organizes learners into what types of intelligences?
  a. Verbal linguistic, mathematical, musically attuned, visual special, body embraced, interpersonal, naturalistic, existential.
  b. Emphatic, recessive, aggressive, assertive, dogmatic, apologetic, determined, elusive.
  c. Verbal linguistic, mathematical logical, musical, visual spatial, body kinesthetic, interpersonal, naturalistic, existential.
  d. Dramatic, musical, verbal, mathematical, dance-oriented, sports-oriented, scientific, socially concerned.

62. Lead teaching, learning centers / learning stations, resource services, team teaching and consultation are all used in:
  a. Innovative teaching
  b. Strategic teaching
  c. Collaborative teaching
  d. Self-contained classrooms

63. A special education teacher has a child who doesn't understand the relationship between ones, tens and hundreds. He is a Bodily Kinesthetic learner. The teacher should:
  a. Draw a colorful chart and put the numbers in the appropriate columns.
  b. Teach him how an abacus works.
  c. Create a song and dance about the numbers families.
  d. Show him the relationship using Monopoly money.

64. Identifying specific skills deficient in special education math students is important so the teacher can decide how to remediate. Problems can include an inability to recall math facts, understand mathematical operations and formulas and how rules are used in solving problems or focusing on attention to details. Such students might be:
  a. Able to solve math problems when they haven't been taught an operation required to do so.
  b. Unable to locate errors in their own work.
  c. Able to solve math problems in another language.
  d. Unable to count higher than 100.

65. What steps are taken to identify specific skill deficits in math?
  a. Standardized assessment tests, examining areas of weakness in student work to determine patterns, teacher observations, interviews with student.
  b. Standardized assessment tests, examining areas of weakness in student work to determine patterns, teacher observations, interviews with parent(s).
  c. Teacher observations coupled with examining areas of weakness in student work are sufficient.
  d. None of the above.

66. A fifth-grade lead teacher and the special education teacher have scheduled a parent conference to discuss the behavior problems of the student. They anticipate the boy's mother will be anxious and defensive as she has been at previous conferences. The best approach for the teachers to take is to:

    a. Draw the parent out about issues in her own life so that she will feel reassured and trusting. Point out possible connections between the mother's emotions about her own life and her son's behaviors and reactions.

    b. Be very firm with the mother, explain the penalties and disciplines her son can expect if the behavior continues and stress neither the parent nor the child has input regarding punishment.

    c. Stress the teachers will not do anything without the parent's approval since they do not want to face liability issues.

    d. Begin by welcoming the mother and telling her about her son's academic improvements. Stress the teachers, the mother and the child share goals for the student's success. Explain the behavior problems and ask if the mother has any insights to share.

67. At the beginning of the week, a special education teacher asked a group of students to generate a list of verbs that make visual or sound pictures. She suggests students think of verbs that mean ways of walking, talking, eating, sitting and playing. The students spend the remainder of the week compiling the list. They notice interesting verbs as they read books, remark on less common verbs they hear in conversation or on television and locate interesting verbs in signs, magazines and other printed materials. One child begins to draw pictures to illustrate some of the verbs. Two children collaborate to create a play in which they demonstrate some of the verbs in a dance. A boy writes a song incorporating the list of verbs. The project is extremely successful. At the end of the week the students have created the following list:

> TIPTOE, SCOOT, MUMBLE, MUNCH, LEAP, SPIN, DIVE, POUNCE, GLIDE, SLITHER, MOAN, WHISPER, GRUMBLE, NIBBLE, SHRILL, HOLLER, PERCH, LEAN, STOMP, MARCH, GIGGLE, HOP, STRUT, SLOUCH, GULP, HOWL, WHINE, SLURP, CROUCH, DRIBBLE, DROOL, HOOT, YELP, YOWL, GROWL, WHISTLE, SHRIEK, SNICKER, INSULT, COMPLIMENT, PLEAD, BARK, WIGGLE, TWIST, SLINK, TODDLE, TRUDGE, WANDER, STROLL.

The teacher's goal is to:

    a. Enhance students' understanding of theme by encouraging them to make connections between categories of verbs.

    b. Enhance students' vocabulary by encouraging them to find examples in the world around them.

    c. Enhance students' understanding of context by encouraging them to explore verbs for contextual clues.

    d. Enhance students' sense of curiosity by directing their attention to a number of different resources they may not have considered.

68. In the previous example, how could the teacher extend the lesson and apply it across the curriculum?
    a. Create a Word Wall with the words the students collected.
    b. Have students work on a class dictionary, putting the words in alphabetical order and explaining what they mean.
    c. Ask students to create a chart noting which verbs have 1, 2 or 3 syllables, which verbs contain double letters, which verbs are also nouns and which verbs have common word-endings.
    d. All of the above.

69. A classroom teacher has a student with learning disabilities that affect her ability to do math. The teacher consults with the special education teacher and decides she will modify the work the child is given by reducing the number of problems, let her have extra time to finish, and provide her with a multiplication chart. The teacher is:
    a. Giving the student an unfair advantage. Letting her have extra time should be sufficient.
    b. Giving the student an unfair advantage. Providing a multiplication chart should be sufficient. With that, she should get her work done on time.
    c. Making appropriate modifications. Each child is different. In this case, she consulted with the special education teacher and concluded the child needs multiple supports.
    d. Modifying the student's work because it makes it easier on the teacher. There is less to explain and less to grade.

70. Explain the philosophy of inclusion.
    a. All children should be included in decisions affecting their education.
    b. Children with special needs are as much a part of the educational community as any other child and necessary services that allow these students to participate in the learning community should be provided.
    c. Parents are part of a child's learning community and should be included in academic decisions.
    d. All teachers and support persons, including Para pros, translators and other assistants, should be allowed to participate in academic decisions.

71. The ADA is:
    a. The Americans with Disabilities Act.
    b. The Anti-Discrimination Act.
    c. The American Diabetes Association.
    d. The Alternatives to Discrimination Act.

72. A teacher working with students who have math disabilities has had success with a variety of multi-sensory techniques including:
    a. Estimating, converting fractions, multiplication families, graphic organizers.
    b. Graphic organizers, math textbooks, multi-step problems, converting fractions.
    c. Memorizing tables, drawing graphs, converting fractions, charting information.
    d. Power point presentations that include music, manipulatives, graphic organizers, clapping games.

73. The development of an IEP is a(n) _____ process.
   a. Indirect.
   b. Collaborative.
   c. Mathematical.
   d. Single.

74. From the age of 3 years to 5 years, a child's expressive vocabulary will usually:
   a. Double
   b. Increase by 25%
   c. Increase by 50%
   d. Triple

75. Which of the following is likely to be most disabling for a young child?
   a. Articulation errors
   b. Hearing loss
   c. Being of below average height
   d. Having slow dentition

Answers and Explanations

1. C: Any device that could help a disabled student in education or life functioning. The Assistive Technology Act of 1998 is the primary legislation regarding assistive technology for disabled students and adults. The act funds 56 state programs concerned with the assistive technology needs of individuals with disabilities. Assistive devices include wheelchairs, hearing aids, glare-reduction screens, Braille devices, voice-recognition software, screen magnifiers and a wealth of other tools.

2. D: He substitutes more enjoyable algebra activities for math drills. Incorporating manipulables such as algebra blocks, math games and applications of algebra to real-life situations, will make math both greater fun and more relevant. When both parent and child are enjoying the work, they will accomplish more in a shorter period of time and the child will feel happy and successful, which encourages her to embrace further learning opportunities.

3. B: Cerebral palsy. Cerebral palsy is an umbrella term that groups neurological childhood disorders that affect muscular control. It does not worsen over time and the cause is located in damaged areas of the brain that control muscle movement. Depending upon the severity of the disorder, a child with cerebral palsy might benefit from an AAC device to help in speaking, forearm crutches to assist in walking or a head pointer for a child whose best motor control is his head.

4. D: Dyscalculia. Dyscalculia defines a range of difficulties in math, such as the inability to understand numbers' meanings, measurements, patterns, mathematical terms and the application of mathematic principals. Early clues include a young child's inability to group items by size or color, recognize patterns or understand the meaning or order of numbers.

5. C: A strategy for diagnosing learning disabilities in which a student with an academic delay receives research-supported interventions to correct the delay. If the interventions do not result in considerable academic improvement, the failure to respond suggests causal learning disabilities.

6. D: Suggest to Alfie that if he is disturbed by Honesty's teasing, he might have a calm, assertive conversation with her in which he tells her he doesn't like it and insist she stop. By encouraging Alfie to act on his own, it shows him he has primary responsibility for taking care of himself. By offering social strategies, he learns a set of skills that will serve him throughout life. If Honesty continues to tease him, he can ask a teacher to step in, but doing so without his invitation is inappropriate.

7. B: Obsessive Compulsive Disorder (OCD). Children and adults with OCD typically engage in a series of highly ritualized behaviors that are rigidly performed when they feel stressed. Behaviors include tapping, snapping fingers, blinking, counting and so forth.

8. A: Intellectual disabilities, hearing, speech, language, visual, orthopedic or other health impairments, emotional disturbance, autism, brain injury caused by trauma, or specific learning disabilities who needs special education and related services. Children with one or

more of these conditions are legally entitled to services and programs designed to help them achieve at the highest level of their ability.

9. D: Students with ADHD are extremely sensitive to distractions. A learning environment in which visual and audio distractions have been eliminated is best. Low lighting, few posters and a clean whiteboard will help minimize distractions.

10. A: Corrective feedback. Corrective feedback is offered to a student in order to explain why a particular error is, in fact, an error. Corrective feedback is specific; it locates where and how the student went astray so that similar errors can be avoided in the future.

11. C: Autism. Autistic children are typically very withdrawn, avoid eye contact and are not responsive to verbal or physical attempts to connect. Some autistic children fall into repetitive behaviors that are very difficult to arrest or prevent. These behaviors include rocking, spinning and handshaking.

12. A: Both, the left. Research using MRIs show dyslexics use both sides of their brains for activities such as reading, while non-dyslexics use only the left side.

13. D: Dysgraphia. Dysgraphic individuals cannot manage the physical act of writing. While many dysgraphics are highly intelligent and able to express themselves cogently, they have extreme difficulty holding a writing implement and shaping letters.

14. B: Increased, persistent thirst. Although there are a number of antidepressants available, most of them share the side effect of a dry, cottony mouth that lasts for a few weeks at the beginning. The student is likely to ask for water frequently because this type of thirst isn't easily quenched. The teacher and the student should understand this side effect will ease and disappear with time.

15. B: With a combination of informal and formal assessments including standardized testing, awareness of grades, systematically charted data over a period of time and teacher notes. Comprehension and vocabulary cannot be sufficiently assessed with occasional, brief studies. Continuous observation, high-stakes and standardized testing, attention to grades and closely tracking the outcomes of objective-linked assessments are interrelated tools that, when systematically organized, offer a solid understanding of students' strengths and weaknesses.

16. A: Diabetic hypoglycemia. Diabetic hypoglycemia, also known as insulin reaction, occurs when blood sugar falls to a very low level. It is important to treat it quickly or the diabetic could faint, in which case an injection of glucagon is administered.

17. D: Enthusiastically accepted. The adults discuss a background check and the possibility the teen might discover gardening is not for her and want to quit. However, this is most likely to occur early in her employment, giving the neighbor sufficient time to find another helper. The teacher is pleased because the girl will learn new skills through modeling and repetition. The mother is pleased because the experience will add to the girl's self-esteem as well as show her she is capable of learning. The elderly neighbor is pleased because she is both compassionate and truly needs help. The girl is delighted the neighbor recognizes her potential and sees her as valuable.

18. C: The student did not know how to spell 'beautiful'. It is doubtful the student heard "pretty" instead of beautiful since the two sound nothing alike. It is equally unlikely he doesn't know the meaning of the word 'beautiful' since his substitution, 'pretty', is a synonym for beautiful. It is likely this child is creative, but that alone wouldn't be sufficient reason to replace one word with another. The most logical answer is that he simply didn't know how to spell 'beautiful'. He does know that some words mean almost the same thing, and since he already knew how to spell 'pretty', he incorrectly believed a synonym would be acceptable.

19. A: Pervasive Spectrum Disorders (PSD) is another name for Autism Spectrum Disorders (ASD). PSD causes disabilities in language, thought, emotion and empathy. The most severe form of PSD is autistic disorder. A much less severe form is Asperger's Syndrome.

20. C: Immediately refer him to the counselor. The boy is exhibiting serious emotional distress suggesting either abuse or neglect at home or elsewhere. While his behavior may seem manipulative, the fact that the boy is unreachable once he's in the highly charged emotional state in which he repeats, "I hate myself" suggests emotional trauma. The fact the child is socialized with peers, playing with them when invited and not taking rejection personally, suggests his emotional distress may be caused by an adult who has convinced him he is unworthy. A trained counselor is the best choice.

21. C: He is socially distant, focused on certain subjects to the point of obsession and inflexible. Asperger Syndrome is a mild form of autism. Children with this disorder typically do interact with teachers, other adults and sometimes other children; however, the interaction is rather remote and without emotional expression. They are also very focused on subjects of great interest to the abandonment of all others. When asked to redirect focus, Asperger children often become emphatically Obstinent, refusing to shift focus.

22. D: All of the above. This project gives the teacher the opportunity to evaluate what students already know, establishes a scaffold of accessible information to which the students can integrate new information and creates a sense of curiosity and excitement in the students, which encourages them to learn.

23. D: A motor skill development disorder which includes speech errors that don't clearly follow a pattern and so appear to be inconsistent. An example is a student who can pronounce /p/ when it is followed by a long i, as in pine, but not when followed by an ou diphthong, as in pout. Verbally dyspraxic individuals are unable to correctly place the tongue, lips and jaw for consistent sounds that can be organized into syllables. Dyspraxia appears to be a brain disorder in which the area that controls production of particular sounds is damaged.

24. B: Ask students to create a play about the story as the teacher reads aloud. This activity grounds the students in the story action as it is occurring. Acting it out insures understanding; otherwise, the students will most likely stop the teacher and ask for clarification. Furthermore, by acting it out, students are incorporating understanding physically. They will be more likely to retain the story and be able to comprehend the meanings incorporated in it.

25. A: Twitches, grunts, inappropriate words, body spasms. Children and adults with Tourette syndrome are rarely aggressive nor are they reluctant to make eye contact or

otherwise engage others. Tourette syndrome is characterized by explosive sounds, sometimes in the form of inappropriate words, more often just as meaningless syllables; muscular twitches of the face or elsewhere in the body and the complete inability to control these spasms. Tourette sufferers often also suffer from Obsessive Compulsive Disorder.

26. C: Lack of sufficiently developed behavior and social skills. The child may or may not be hyperactive, but the fact that she can control her behavior for extended periods if a reward is involved suggests the child is overly indulged outside of class. In addition, she appears to act out in an effort to seek peer admiration; this excludes the possibility of Tourette syndrome and Attention Deficit Hyperactivity Disorder. In the first case, she would be unlikely to seek approval. In the second, she would be unlikely to be able to control herself under certain circumstances. There is nothing in her behavior to suggest psychosis.

27. A: Attention Deficit Hyperactivity Disorder. Children with ADHD exhibit a myriad of symptoms including: disorganization, easily distracted and frustrated, defensive, immature, impulsive, often interrupts conversations and hyperactive behaviors.

28. A: Reading fluency. Fluent readers are able to read smoothly and comfortably at a steady pace. The more quickly a child reads, the greater the chance of leaving out a word or substituting one word for another, i.e., wink instead of *sink*. Fluent readers are able to maintain accuracy without sacrificing rate. Fluent readers also stress important words in a text, group words into rhythmic phrases and read with intonation (prosody).

29. B: Drink a soda or eat some hard candy. Diabetes is a metabolic disorder that prevents proper processing of food, resulting in a lack of enough insulin for the blood to transport sugar. Insulin shock, also known as hypoglycemia, is typically brought on by a diabetic's failure to take insulin or to eat often enough. It is a serious condition that must be dealt with immediately.

30. D: A and B. Any opportunity for an ELL to hear spoken English while simultaneously seeing it in print will help facilitate reading fluency.

31. B: The classroom teacher, a special education teacher, parents or guardian, a representative of the local education agency knowledgeable about specialized instruction, someone to interpret instructional implications, the student if appropriate and other people invited by the parents or the school. IDEA defines the IEP team as a group of people responsible for developing, reviewing and revising the Individualized Education Program for a disabled student.

32. C: Reading at a Frustration reading level. At a Frustration reading level, a student is unable to unlock meaning from a text regardless of teacher support or strategies. The reader is at this level when he has less than 90% accuracy in word recognition and less than 50% in comprehension, retelling a story is illogical or incomplete and the student cannot accurately answer questions about the text.

33. B: Understanding of context and vocabulary. A Cloze test presents a reader with a text in which certain words are blocked out. The reader must determine probable missing words based on context clues. In order to supply these words, the reader must already know them.

34. A: Letter-sound correspondence. Letter-sound correspondence is the relationship between a spoken sound and the letters predictably used in English to transcribe them.

35. D: Memorize their lists by using techniques such as songs, mnemonic devices and other fun activities. By definition, sight words cannot be decoded but must be recognized on sight.

36. A: Oral. Phonological awareness is the understanding of the sounds within a spoken word. While phonological awareness contributes to fluent reading skills, activities designed to develop an awareness of word-sounds are, by definition, oral.

37. A: Count money, plan meals, grocery shop, recognize safety concerns. These are among the most basic life skills developmentally delayed students must master. Other life skills include specific occupational skills, home maintenance, clothes selection and care, food preparation and personal hygiene.

38. A: Word recognition. Elements of word recognition include strategies to decode unfamiliar words, considering alternate word meanings to decode a text and the ability to apply prior knowledge to determine a word's meaning.

39. A: Scripting the end-sound to a word KT=cat; leaving space between words; writing from the top left to the top right and from top to bottom of the page. Each of these steps is progressively more abstract. Scripting the end-sound to a word helps a young writer recognize words have beginnings and endings. This naturally leads to the willingness to separate words with white space so they stand as individual entities. Once this step is reached, the child realizes English, writing progresses from left to right and from the top of the page to the bottom.

40. A: Are results-oriented, includes post-school activities, vocational education, employment support, adult services and considers the individual's strengths, preferences and interests. Additional activities that compose Secondary Transition are instruction, related services, community experiences, the development of employment and other post-school adult living objectives and, if appropriate, acquisition of daily living skills and functional vocational evaluation.

41. B: Suggesting they read their stories to other students. Emergent writers scripting initial and final sounds will gain the most immediate and relevant satisfaction by moving around the room, reading what they've written to other students.

42. D: From the first day of school. Picture walks give young readers the idea books are arranged sequentially. Pictures provide narrative coherence and context clues. Holding a book and turning pages gives young readers a familiarity with them.

43. D: Students should be taught that writing is a process. By applying spelling patterns found in word families, the spelling of many words can be deduced.

44. C: Context. By considering the other words in the story, the student can deduce the missing words. Referring to other words when a reader encounters an unfamiliar or missing word, can often unlock meaning.

45. A: Cooperative learning and reading comprehension. CSR is group of four reading strategies that students with learning disabilities can use to decipher and understand texts. Small groups of students at various reading levels support one another by going through the strategies as they read aloud or silently. Before reading, the group *previews*, applying prior knowledge and prediction. Next readers target words or syllables they didn't understand called *clunks* and apply a number of strategies to decode the *clunks.* Third, students *get the gist* by determining the most important character, setting, event or idea. Finally, the students *wrap it up* by creating questions to discuss their understanding of the text and summarize its meaning.

46. B: Have an Individualized Education Plan written for her. An IEP is a requirement of law. The plan, written by a team of individuals including her classroom teacher, the special education teacher, her parent s, the student if appropriate and other interested individuals, establishes objectives and goals and offers a time-line in which to reach them.

47. C: Observe the child over the course of a week or two. Draw him into conversation to determine if vocabulary is limited. Note how the child interacts with others in the class. Does he initiate conversation? If another child initiates, does he respond? Once the teacher has observed, she is in a better position to offer information to the special education teacher or counselor and to determine her best course of action.

48. B: Meet with the specialist to discuss the teacher's goals. It isn't possible to determine if strategies are effective or determine a future course unless the teacher has a firm grasp of his goals and expectations.

49. A: Strategies to increase comprehension and to build vocabulary. He should receive instruction focused on just the areas in which he is exhibiting difficulty. Improved vocabulary will give him greater comprehension skills. Strategies focused on enhancing comprehension together with a stronger vocabulary will provide the greatest help.

50. A: It enhances students' phonemic awareness and increases vocabulary. Strength in oral language helps emergent readers because reading relies largely upon the ability to decode words with knowledge about what sounds the letters represent. A large vocabulary helps the reader recognize words whose sounds are properly decoded but whose meanings aren't familiar. Unfamiliar words slow reading fluency.

51. B: Scaffolding. Scaffolding is an umbrella teaching approach which offers a multitude of supports. Scaffolding includes prior knowledge, mnemonic devices, modeling, graphs, charts, graphic organizers and information needed prior to starting the lesson such as vocabulary or mathematical formulas.

52. D: Visit the classroom, meet the teacher and her new classmates and be given the opportunity to ask questions about the change she is about to make. When she is able to visualize what the classroom looks like, meet the people that will become her new educational 'family' and have her concerns and questions addressed, she will feel more confident about the transition.

53. B: A Maze test, which is a type of Cloze test. A Cloze test offers a text with key words blanked out and the student must determine the most likely words based upon context and

his vocabulary. A Maze test offers a number of possible answers and the student must read very carefully in order to make the correct selection.

54. C: Use graph paper to help him organize. Show him how to write the problems, keeping each number in a box aligned with other numbers. This will help him determine which numbers are in the ones group, the tens group, the hundreds group and so on.

55. B: Muscular dystrophy. There are 20 types of muscular dystrophy, a genetically inherited disease that frequently first manifests in childhood. By contrast, muscular sclerosis almost never appears in childhood. Cerebral palsy is not a deteriorating disease, as is muscular dystrophy.

56. C: One class at a time, with the special education teacher supervising his academic and social progress. It is important to make this transition slowly, to permit the special education teacher to remain in the student's life as both academic and emotional support and the student to adjust to her larger classes and students she doesn't know as well.

57. C: Outreach to underrepresented and rural populations. The four required activities of the AT ACT of 1998 are: a public awareness program, coordinate activities among state agencies, technical assistance and training and outreach to underrepresented and rural populations.

58. B: Positive Behavior Support. The Individuals with Disabilities Education Act of 1997 is the recommended method of dealing with behavioral problems in children with disabilities.

59. C: Assessing a young child for learning disabilities often leads to an incorrect conclusion because a student must be taught the subject before it is possible to assess her understanding of it. Intervention teaches the child specific skills to correct her misconceptions. If the intervention fails, assessment is the next step. Many experts recommend such assessment should not be undertaken until a child is at least six years of age.

60. B: Least restrictive. IDEA requires the least restrictive environment (LRE) appropriate to a child's needs is the proper learning environment so children are not unnecessarily isolated from non-disabled children. The student's IEP team is responsible for determining the LRE.

61. C: Verbal linguistic, mathematical logical, musical, visual spatial, body kinesthetic, interpersonal, naturalistic, existential. Harvard Professor Howard Gardner cites his theory of multiple intelligences, also called learning styles, as an answer to how teachers can most effectively reach all their students. It is especially important to recognize the learning styles of students with learning disabilities and design lessons for those students accordingly.

62. C: Collaborative teaching. Classrooms with a lead teacher often include a specialized teacher to listen to the lesson then work with special needs children. Other methods are: learning centers or stations in which collaborating teachers are responsible for different areas, assigning special needs students into a resource room, team teaching and/or consultation by the special education teacher to the classroom teacher.

63. B: Teach him how an abacus works. An abacus gives both a visual/tactile demonstration of how numbers work and allows a child who processes information through hand/body movement to physically experience numerical relationships.

64. B: Unable to locate errors in their own work. This is the only logical answer. Answers a, c and d do not make sense in context.

65. A: Standardized assessment tests, examining areas of weakness in student work to determine patterns, teacher observations and interviews with the student. At this point the teacher is well-prepared to plan instruction.

66. D: Begin by welcoming the mother and discussing her son's academic improvements. Stress that the teachers, the mother and the child share goals for the student's success. Explain the behavior problems and ask if the mother has insights to share. It's important to keep communication open.

67. B: Enhance students' vocabulary by encouraging them to find examples in the world around them. Often children have richer vocabularies than they realize. This project simultaneously encourages students to remember words they already know and to learn other words with similar meanings.

68. D: All of the above. There is often a multitude of ways a teacher can apply skills and information learned in one lesson to other subjects. In this case, vocabulary building is enhanced with a word wall; logic and reasoning skills are developed by putting the words into alphabetical order then carefully considering how to define them; and both math skills and word recognition ability are improved by creating a chart demonstrating a variety of ways one can categorize a list of words.

69. C: Making appropriate modifications. Each child is different. In this case, she has consulted with the special education teacher and concluded the child needs multiple supports.

70. B: Children with special needs are as much a part of the educational community as any other child and necessary services that allow these students to participate in the learning community should be provided.

71. A: The Americans with Disabilities Act. The ADA is a federal act prohibiting discrimination based on disability in the areas of employment, state and local government, public accommodations, commercial facilities, transportation and telecommunications.

72. D: Power point presentations that include music, manipulatives, graphic organizers and clapping games. Multi-sensory techniques include visual, audio, tactile and kinesthetic approaches to teaching.

73. B: Collaborative. The creation of an Individualized Education Plan (IEP) involves classroom and special education teachers, family members, the student (if appropriate) and other interested parties who collaborate in the student's best interests.

74. C: From the age of 3 years to 5 years, a child's spoken vocabulary will typically increase by 50% (c). A typical 3-year-old will have a maximum expressive vocabulary of around

1,000 words*; by age 5, this will have increased to around 1,500 words. (*Children develop vocabularies of around 300 to 1,000 words in their first three years; the increase percentage here is based on the high end.) Vocabulary development is more rapid from age 1 to 3 since the child is starting from nothing and has more words to learn. If the child's earlier development has been optimal, the additional increase in spoken vocabulary by age 5 is 50%, making (a), (b), and (d) incorrect.

75. B: Having hearing loss (b) is likely to be most disabling for a young child as it will interfere with language and speech development. The drive to have universal newborn hearing screenings is based on statistics showing that children's academic progress is significantly impeded by hearing loss. Even when hearing loss is mild, children are much more likely to fail a school grade later without early intervention. Articulation errors (a) are quite common in young children and are generally resolved as children learn to speak. The norms for correct articulation of various speech sounds range from roughly ages 7 to 9, so 3- to 6-year-olds are likely to make articulation errors. Being of below average height (c) is not as disabling as hearing loss. Short stature has some social implications in older children, but has less impact in early childhood. There is enough natural variation in children's heights that it is normal to be shorter or taller than peers. Having slow dentition (d) means the child's teeth take longer than average to erupt; this is not significantly disabling like hearing loss.

Secret Key #1 - Time is Your Greatest Enemy

Pace Yourself

Wear a watch. At the beginning of the test, check the time (or start a chronometer on your watch to count the minutes), and check the time after every few questions to make sure you are "on schedule."

If you are forced to speed up, do it efficiently. Usually one or more answer choices can be eliminated without too much difficulty. Above all, don't panic. Don't speed up and just begin guessing at random choices. By pacing yourself, and continually monitoring your progress against your watch, you will always know exactly how far ahead or behind you are with your available time. If you find that you are one minute behind on the test, don't skip one question without spending any time on it, just to catch back up. Take 15 fewer seconds on the next four questions, and after four questions you'll have caught back up. Once you catch back up, you can continue working each problem at your normal pace.

Furthermore, don't dwell on the problems that you were rushed on. If a problem was taking up too much time and you made a hurried guess, it must be difficult. The difficult questions are the ones you are most likely to miss anyway, so it isn't a big loss. It is better to end with more time than you need than to run out of time.

Lastly, sometimes it is beneficial to slow down if you are constantly getting ahead of time. You are always more likely to catch a careless mistake by working more slowly than quickly, and among very high-scoring test takers (those who are likely to have lots of time left over), careless errors affect the score more than mastery of material.

Secret Key #2 - Guessing is not Guesswork

You probably know that guessing is a good idea. Unlike other standardized tests, there is no penalty for getting a wrong answer. Even if you have no idea about a question, you still have a 20-25% chance of getting it right.

Most test takers do not understand the impact that proper guessing can have on their score. Unless you score extremely high, guessing will significantly contribute to your final score.

Monkeys Take the Test

What most test takers don't realize is that to insure that 20-25% chance, you have to guess randomly. If you put 20 monkeys in a room to take this test, assuming they answered once per question and behaved themselves, on average they would get 20-25% of the questions correct. Put 20 test takers in the room, and the average will be much lower among guessed questions. Why?
    1. The test writers intentionally write deceptive answer choices that "look" right. A test

taker has no idea about a question, so he picks the "best looking" answer, which is often wrong. The monkey has no idea what looks good and what doesn't, so it will consistently be right about 20-25% of the time.

2. Test takers will eliminate answer choices from the guessing pool based on a hunch or intuition. Simple but correct answers often get excluded, leaving a 0% chance of being correct. The monkey has no clue, and often gets lucky with the best choice.

This is why the process of elimination endorsed by most test courses is flawed and detrimental to your performance. Test takers don't guess; they make an ignorant stab in the dark that is usually worse than random.

$5 Challenge

Let me introduce one of the most valuable ideas of this course—the $5 challenge:

You only mark your "best guess" if you are willing to bet $5 on it.
You only eliminate choices from guessing if you are willing to bet $5 on it.

Why $5? Five dollars is an amount of money that is small yet not insignificant, and can really add up fast (20 questions could cost you $100). Likewise, each answer choice on one question of the test will have a small impact on your overall score, but it can really add up to a lot of points in the end.

The process of elimination IS valuable. The following shows your chance of guessing it right:

If you eliminate wrong answer choices until only this many remain:	Chance of getting it correct:
1	100%
2	50%
3	33%

However, if you accidentally eliminate the right answer or go on a hunch for an incorrect answer, your chances drop dramatically—to 0%. By guessing among all the answer choices, you are GUARANTEED to have a shot at the right answer.

That's why the $5 test is so valuable. If you give up the advantage and safety of a pure guess, it had better be worth the risk.

What we still haven't covered is how to be sure that whatever guess you make is truly random. Here's the easiest way:

Always pick the first answer choice among those remaining.

Such a technique means that you have decided, **before you see a single test question**, exactly how you are going to guess, and since the order of choices tells you nothing about which one is correct, this guessing technique is perfectly random.

This section is not meant to scare you away from making educated guesses or eliminating choices; you just need to define when a choice is worth eliminating. The $5 test, along with a pre-defined random guessing strategy, is the best way to make sure you reap all of the benefits of guessing.

Secret Key #3 - Practice Smarter, Not Harder

Many test takers delay the test preparation process because they dread the awful amounts of practice time they think necessary to succeed on the test. We have refined an effective method that will take you only a fraction of the time.

There are a number of "obstacles" in the path to success. Among these are answering questions, finishing in time, and mastering test-taking strategies. All must be executed on the day of the test at peak performance, or your score will suffer. The test is a mental marathon that has a large impact on your future.

Just like a marathon runner, it is important to work your way up to the full challenge. So first you just worry about questions, and then time, and finally strategy:

Success Strategy

1. Find a good source for practice tests.
2. If you are willing to make a larger time investment, consider using more than one study guide. Often the different approaches of multiple authors will help you "get" difficult concepts.
3. Take a practice test with no time constraints, with all study helps, "open book." Take your time with questions and focus on applying strategies.
4. Take a practice test with time constraints, with all guides, "open book."
5. Take a final practice test without open material and with time limits.

If you have time to take more practice tests, just repeat step 5. By gradually exposing yourself to the full rigors of the test environment, you will condition your mind to the stress of test day and maximize your success.

Secret Key #4 - Prepare, Don't Procrastinate

Let me state an obvious fact: if you take the test three times, you will probably get three different scores. This is due to the way you feel on test day, the level of preparedness you have, and the version of the test you see. Despite the test writers' claims to the contrary, some versions of the test WILL be easier for you than others.

Since your future depends so much on your score, you should maximize your chances of success. In order to maximize the likelihood of success, you've got to prepare in advance.

This means taking practice tests and spending time learning the information and test taking strategies you will need to succeed.

Never go take the actual test as a "practice" test, expecting that you can just take it again if you need to. Take all the practice tests you can on your own, but when you go to take the official test, be prepared, be focused, and do your best the first time!

Secret Key #5 - Test Yourself

Everyone knows that time is money. There is no need to spend too much of your time or too little of your time preparing for the test. You should only spend as much of your precious time preparing as is necessary for you to get the score you need.

Once you have taken a practice test under real conditions of time constraints, then you will know if you are ready for the test or not.

If you have scored extremely high the first time that you take the practice test, then there is not much point in spending countless hours studying. You are already there.

Benchmark your abilities by retaking practice tests and seeing how much you have improved. Once you consistently score high enough to guarantee success, then you are ready.

If you have scored well below where you need, then knuckle down and begin studying in earnest. Check your improvement regularly through the use of practice tests under real conditions. Above all, don't worry, panic, or give up. The key is perseverance!

Then, when you go to take the test, remain confident and remember how well you did on the practice tests. If you can score high enough on a practice test, then you can do the same on the real thing.

General Strategies

The most important thing you can do is to ignore your fears and jump into the test immediately. Do not be overwhelmed by any strange-sounding terms. You have to jump into the test like jumping into a pool—all at once is the easiest way.

Make Predictions

As you read and understand the question, try to guess what the answer will be. Remember that several of the answer choices are wrong, and once you begin reading them, your mind will immediately become cluttered with answer choices designed to throw you off. Your mind is typically the most focused immediately after you have read the question and digested its contents. If you can, try to predict what the correct answer will be. You may be surprised at what you can predict.

Quickly scan the choices and see if your prediction is in the listed answer choices. If it is, then you can be quite confident that you have the right answer. It still won't hurt to check the other answer choices, but most of the time, you've got it!

Answer the Question

It may seem obvious to only pick answer choices that answer the question, but the test writers can create some excellent answer choices that are wrong. Don't pick an answer just because it sounds right, or you believe it to be true. It MUST answer the question. Once you've made your selection, always go back and check it against the question and make sure that you didn't misread the question and that the answer choice does answer the question posed.

Benchmark

After you read the first answer choice, decide if you think it sounds correct or not. If it doesn't, move on to the next answer choice. If it does, mentally mark that answer choice. This doesn't mean that you've definitely selected it as your answer choice, it just means that it's the best you've seen thus far. Go ahead and read the next choice. If the next choice is worse than the one you've already selected, keep going to the next answer choice. If the next choice is better than the choice you've already selected, mentally mark the new answer choice as your best guess.

The first answer choice that you select becomes your standard. Every other answer choice must be benchmarked against that standard. That choice is correct until proven otherwise by another answer choice beating it out. Once you've decided that no other answer choice seems as good, do one final check to ensure that your answer choice answers the question posed.

Valid Information

Don't discount any of the information provided in the question. Every piece of information may be necessary to determine the correct answer. None of the information in the question is there to throw you off (while the answer choices will certainly have information to throw you off). If two seemingly unrelated topics are discussed, don't ignore either. You can be confident there is a relationship, or it wouldn't be included in the question, and you are probably going to have to determine what is that relationship to find the answer.

Avoid "Fact Traps"

Don't get distracted by a choice that is factually true. Your search is for the answer that answers the question. Stay focused and don't fall for an answer that is true but irrelevant. Always go back to the question and make sure you're choosing an answer that actually answers the question and is not just a true statement. An answer can be factually correct, but it MUST answer the question asked. Additionally, two answers can both be seemingly correct, so be sure to read all of the answer choices, and make sure that you get the one that BEST answers the question.

Milk the Question

Some of the questions may throw you completely off. They might deal with a subject you have not been exposed to, or one that you haven't reviewed in years. While your lack of knowledge about the subject will be a hindrance, the question itself can give you many clues that will help you find the correct answer. Read the question carefully and look for clues. Watch particularly for adjectives and nouns describing difficult terms or words that you don't recognize. Regardless of whether you completely understand a word or not, replacing it with a synonym, either provided or one you more familiar with, may help you to understand what the questions are asking. Rather than wracking your mind about specific detailed information concerning a difficult term or word, try to use mental substitutes that are easier to understand.

The Trap of Familiarity

Don't just choose a word because you recognize it. On difficult questions, you may not recognize a number of words in the answer choices. The test writers don't put "make-believe" words on the test, so don't think that just because you only recognize all the words in one answer choice that that answer choice must be correct. If you only recognize words in one answer choice, then focus on that one. Is it correct? Try your best to determine if it is correct. If it is, that's great. If not, eliminate it. Each word and answer choice you eliminate increases your chances of getting the question correct, even if you then have to guess among the unfamiliar choices.

Eliminate Answers

Eliminate choices as soon as you realize they are wrong. But be careful! Make sure you consider all of the possible answer choices. Just because one appears right, doesn't mean that the next one won't be even better! The test writers will usually put more than one good answer choice for every question, so read all of them. Don't worry if you are stuck between two that seem right. By getting down to just two remaining possible choices, your odds are now 50/50. Rather than wasting too much time, play the odds. You are guessing, but guessing wisely because you've been able to knock out some of the answer choices that you know are wrong. If you are eliminating choices and realize that the last answer choice you are left with is also obviously wrong, don't panic. Start over and consider each choice again. There may easily be something that you missed the first time and will realize on the second pass.

Tough Questions

If you are stumped on a problem or it appears too hard or too difficult, don't waste time. Move on! Remember though, if you can quickly check for obviously incorrect answer choices, your chances of guessing correctly are greatly improved. Before you completely give up, at least try to knock out a couple of possible answers. Eliminate what you can and then guess at the remaining answer choices before moving on.

Brainstorm

If you get stuck on a difficult question, spend a few seconds quickly brainstorming. Run through the complete list of possible answer choices. Look at each choice and ask yourself, "Could this answer the question satisfactorily?" Go through each answer choice and consider it independently of the others. By systematically going through all possibilities, you may find something that you would otherwise overlook. Remember though that when you get stuck, it's important to try to keep moving.

Read Carefully

Understand the problem. Read the question and answer choices carefully. Don't miss the question because you misread the terms. You have plenty of time to read each question thoroughly and make sure you understand what is being asked. Yet a happy medium must be attained, so don't waste too much time. You must read carefully, but efficiently.

Face Value

When in doubt, use common sense. Always accept the situation in the problem at face value. Don't read too much into it. These problems will not require you to make huge leaps of logic. The test writers aren't trying to throw you off with a cheap trick. If you have to go beyond creativity and make a leap of logic in order to have an answer choice answer the question, then you should look at the other answer choices. Don't overcomplicate the problem by creating theoretical relationships or explanations that will warp time or space. These are normal problems rooted in reality. It's just that the applicable relationship or explanation may not be readily apparent and you have to figure things out. Use your common sense to interpret anything that isn't clear.

Prefixes

If you're having trouble with a word in the question or answer choices, try dissecting it. Take advantage of every clue that the word might include. Prefixes and suffixes can be a huge help. Usually they allow you to determine a basic meaning. Pre- means before, post- means after, pro - is positive, de- is negative. From these prefixes and suffixes, you can get an idea of the general meaning of the word and try to put it into context. Beware though of any traps. Just because con- is the opposite of pro-, doesn't necessarily mean congress is the opposite of progress!

Hedge Phrases

Watch out for critical hedge phrases, led off with words such as "likely," "may," "can," "sometimes," "often," "almost," "mostly," "usually," "generally," "rarely," and "sometimes." Question writers insert these hedge phrases to cover every possibility. Often an answer choice will be wrong simply because it leaves no room for exception. Unless the situation calls for them, avoid answer choices that have definitive words like "exactly," and "always."

Switchback Words

Stay alert for "switchbacks." These are the words and phrases frequently used to alert you to shifts in thought. The most common switchback word is "but." Others include "although," "however," "nevertheless," "on the other hand," "even though," "while," "in spite of," "despite," and "regardless of."

New Information

Correct answer choices will rarely have completely new information included. Answer choices typically are straightforward reflections of the material asked about and will directly relate to the question. If a new piece of information is included in an answer choice that doesn't even seem to relate to the topic being asked about, then that answer choice is likely incorrect. All of the information needed to answer the question is usually provided for you in the question. You should not have to make guesses that are unsupported or choose answer choices that require unknown information that cannot be reasoned from what is given.

Time Management

On technical questions, don't get lost on the technical terms. Don't spend too much time on any one question. If you don't know what a term means, then odds are you aren't going to get much further since you don't have a dictionary. You should be able to immediately recognize whether or not you know a term. If you don't, work with the other clues that you have—the other answer choices and terms provided—but don't waste too much time trying to figure out a difficult term that you don't know.

Contextual Clues

Look for contextual clues. An answer can be right but not the correct answer. The contextual clues will help you find the answer that is most right and is correct. Understand the context in which a phrase or statement is made. This will help you make important distinctions.

Don't Panic

Panicking will not answer any questions for you; therefore, it isn't helpful. When you first see the question, if your mind goes blank, take a deep breath. Force yourself to mechanically go through the steps of solving the problem using the strategies you've learned.

Pace Yourself

Don't get clock fever. It's easy to be overwhelmed when you're looking at a page full of questions, your mind is full of random thoughts and feeling confused, and the clock is ticking down faster than you would like. Calm down and maintain the pace that you have set for yourself. As long as you are on track by monitoring your pace, you are guaranteed to have enough time for yourself. When you get to the last few minutes of the test, it may seem like you won't have enough time left, but if you only have as many questions as you should have left at that point, then you're right on track!

Answer Selection

The best way to pick an answer choice is to eliminate all of those that are wrong, until only one is left and confirm that is the correct answer. Sometimes though, an answer choice may immediately look right. Be careful! Take a second to make sure that the other choices are not equally obvious. Don't make a hasty mistake. There are only two times that you should stop before checking other answers. First is when you are positive that the answer choice you have selected is correct. Second is when time is almost out and you have to make a quick guess!

Check Your Work

Since you will probably not know every term listed and the answer to every question, it is important that you get credit for the ones that you do know. Don't miss any questions through careless mistakes. If at all possible, try to take a second to look back over your answer selection and make sure you've selected the correct answer choice and haven't made a costly careless mistake (such as marking an answer choice that you didn't mean to mark). The time it takes for this quick double check should more than pay for itself in caught mistakes.

Beware of Directly Quoted Answers

Sometimes an answer choice will repeat word for word a portion of the question or reference section. However, beware of such exact duplication. It may be a trap! More than likely, the correct choice will paraphrase or summarize a point, rather than being exactly the same wording.

Slang

Scientific sounding answers are better than slang ones. An answer choice that begins "To compare the outcomes..." is much more likely to be correct than one that begins "Because some people insisted..."

Extreme Statements

Avoid wild answers that throw out highly controversial ideas that are proclaimed as established fact. An answer choice that states the "process should used in certain situations, if..." is much more likely to be correct than one that states the "process should be discontinued completely." The first is a calm rational statement and doesn't even make a definitive, uncompromising stance, using a hedge word "if" to provide wiggle room, whereas the second choice is a radical idea and far more extreme.

Answer Choice Families

When you have two or more answer choices that are direct opposites or parallels, one of them is usually the correct answer. For instance, if one answer choice states "x increases" and another answer choice states "x decreases" or "y increases," then those two or three answer choices are very similar in construction and fall into the same family of answer choices. A family of answer choices consists of two or three answer choices, very similar in construction, but often with directly opposite meanings. Usually the correct answer choice will be in that family of answer choices. The "odd man out" or answer choice that doesn't seem to fit the parallel construction of the other answer choices is more likely to be incorrect.

Special Report: How to Overcome Test Anxiety

The very nature of tests caters to some level of anxiety, nervousness, or tension, just as we feel for any important event that occurs in our lives. A little bit of anxiety or nervousness can be a good thing. It helps us with motivation, and makes achievement just that much sweeter. However, too much anxiety can be a problem, especially if it hinders our ability to function and perform.

"Test anxiety," is the term that refers to the emotional reactions that some test-takers experience when faced with a test or exam. Having a fear of testing and exams is based upon a rational fear, since the test-taker's performance can shape the course of an academic career. Nevertheless, experiencing excessive fear of examinations will only interfere with the test-taker's ability to perform and chance to be successful.

There are a large variety of causes that can contribute to the development and sensation of test anxiety. These include, but are not limited to, lack of preparation and worrying about issues surrounding the test.

Lack of Preparation

Lack of preparation can be identified by the following behaviors or situations:

Not scheduling enough time to study, and therefore cramming the night before the test or exam
Managing time poorly, to create the sensation that there is not enough time to do everything
Failing to organize the text information in advance, so that the study material consists of the entire text and not simply the pertinent information
Poor overall studying habits

Worrying, on the other hand, can be related to both the test taker, or many other factors around him/her that will be affected by the results of the test. These include worrying about:

Previous performances on similar exams, or exams in general
How friends and other students are achieving
The negative consequences that will result from a poor grade or failure

There are three primary elements to test anxiety. Physical components, which involve the same typical bodily reactions as those to acute anxiety (to be discussed below). Emotional factors have to do with fear or panic. Mental or cognitive issues concerning attention spans and memory abilities.

Physical Signals

There are many different symptoms of test anxiety, and these are not limited to mental and emotional strain. Frequently there are a range of physical signals that will let a test taker know that he/she is suffering from test anxiety. These bodily changes can include the following:

Perspiring
Sweaty palms
Wet, trembling hands
Nausea
Dry mouth
A knot in the stomach
Headache
Faintness
Muscle tension
Aching shoulders, back and neck
Rapid heart beat
Feeling too hot/cold

To recognize the sensation of test anxiety, a test-taker should monitor him/herself for the following sensations:

The physical distress symptoms as listed above
Emotional sensitivity, expressing emotional feelings such as the need to cry or laugh too much, or a sensation of anger or helplessness
A decreased ability to think, causing the test-taker to blank out or have racing thoughts that are hard to organize or control.

Though most students will feel some level of anxiety when faced with a test or exam, the majority can cope with that anxiety and maintain it at a manageable level. However, those who cannot are faced with a very real and very serious condition, which can and should be controlled for the immeasurable benefit of this sufferer.

Naturally, these sensations lead to negative results for the testing experience. The most common effects of test anxiety have to do with nervousness and mental blocking.

Nervousness

Nervousness can appear in several different levels:

The test-taker's difficulty, or even inability to read and understand the questions on the test
The difficulty or inability to organize thoughts to a coherent form
The difficulty or inability to recall key words and concepts relating to the testing questions (especially essays)
The receipt of poor grades on a test, though the test material was well known by the test taker

Conversely, a person may also experience mental blocking, which involves:

Blanking out on test questions
Only remembering the correct answers to the questions when the test has already finished.

Fortunately for test anxiety sufferers, beating these feelings, to a large degree, has to do with proper preparation. When a test taker has a feeling of preparedness, then anxiety will be dramatically lessened.

The first step to resolving anxiety issues is to distinguish which of the two types of anxiety are being suffered. If the anxiety is a direct result of a lack of preparation, this should be considered a normal reaction, and the anxiety level (as opposed to the test results) shouldn't be anything to worry about. However, if, when adequately prepared, the test-taker still panics, blanks out, or seems to overreact, this is not a fully rational reaction. While this can be considered normal too, there are many ways to combat and overcome these effects.

Remember that anxiety cannot be entirely eliminated, however, there are ways to minimize it, to make the anxiety easier to manage. Preparation is one of the best ways to minimize test anxiety. Therefore the following techniques are wise in order to best fight off any anxiety that may want to build.

To begin with, try to avoid cramming before a test, whenever it is possible. By trying to memorize an entire term's worth of information in one day, you'll be shocking your system, and not giving yourself a very good chance to absorb the information. This is an easy path to anxiety, so for those who suffer from test anxiety, cramming should not even be considered an option.

Instead of cramming, work throughout the semester to combine all of the material which is presented throughout the semester, and work on it gradually as the course goes by, making sure to master the main concepts first, leaving minor details for a week or so before the test.

To study for the upcoming exam, be sure to pose questions that may be on the examination, to gauge the ability to answer them by integrating the ideas from your texts, notes and lectures, as well as any supplementary readings.

If it is truly impossible to cover all of the information that was covered in that particular term, concentrate on the most important portions, that can be covered very well. Learn these concepts as best as possible, so that when the test comes, a goal can be made to use these concepts as presentations of your knowledge.

In addition to study habits, changes in attitude are critical to beating a struggle with test anxiety. In fact, an improvement of the perspective over the entire test-taking experience can actually help a test taker to enjoy studying and therefore improve the overall experience. Be certain not to overemphasize the significance of the grade - know that the result of the test is neither a reflection of self worth, nor is it a measure of intelligence; one grade will not predict a person's future success.

To improve an overall testing outlook, the following steps should be tried:

Keeping in mind that the most reasonable expectation for taking a test is to expect to try to demonstrate as much of what you know as you possibly can.
Reminding ourselves that a test is only one test; this is not the only one, and there will be others.
The thought of thinking of oneself in an irrational, all-or-nothing term should be avoided at all costs.
A reward should be designated for after the test, so there's something to look forward to. Whether it be going to a movie, going out to eat, or simply visiting friends, schedule it in advance, and do it no matter what result is expected on the exam.

Test-takers should also keep in mind that the basics are some of the most important things, even beyond anti-anxiety techniques and studying. Never neglect the basic social, emotional and biological needs, in order to try to absorb information. In order to best achieve, these three factors must be held as just as important as the studying itself.

Study Steps

Remember the following important steps for studying:

Maintain healthy nutrition and exercise habits. Continue both your recreational activities and social pass times. These both contribute to your physical and emotional well being.
Be certain to get a good amount of sleep, especially the night before the test, because when you're overtired you are not able to perform to the best of your best ability.
Keep the studying pace to a moderate level by taking breaks when they are needed, and varying the work whenever possible, to keep the mind fresh instead of getting bored. When enough studying has been done that all the material that can be learned has been learned, and the test taker is prepared for the test, stop studying and do something relaxing such as listening to music, watching a movie, or taking a warm bubble bath.

There are also many other techniques to minimize the uneasiness or apprehension that is experienced along with test anxiety before, during, or even after the examination. In fact, there are a great deal of things that can be done to stop anxiety from interfering with lifestyle and performance. Again, remember that anxiety will not be eliminated entirely, and it shouldn't be. Otherwise that "up" feeling for exams would not exist, and most of us depend on that sensation to perform better than usual. However, this anxiety has to be at a level that is manageable.

Of course, as we have just discussed, being prepared for the exam is half the battle right away. Attending all classes, finding out what knowledge will be expected on the exam, and knowing the exam schedules are easy steps to lowering anxiety. Keeping up with work will remove the need to cram, and efficient study habits will eliminate wasted time. Studying should be done in an ideal location for concentration, so that it is simple to become interested in the material and give it complete attention. A method such as SQ3R (Survey, Question, Read, Recite, Review) is a wonderful key to follow to make sure that the study habits are as effective as possible, especially in the case of learning from a textbook. Flashcards are great techniques for memorization. Learning to take good notes will mean that notes will be full of useful information, so that less sifting will need to be done to seek out what is pertinent for studying. Reviewing notes after class and then again on occasion will keep the information fresh in the mind. From notes that have been taken summary sheets and outlines can be made for simpler reviewing.

A study group can also be a very motivational and helpful place to study, as there will be a sharing of ideas, all of the minds can work together, to make sure that everyone understands, and the studying will be made more interesting because it will be a social occasion.

Basically, though, as long as the test-taker remains organized and self confident, with efficient study habits, less time will need to be spent studying, and higher grades will be achieved.

To become self confident, there are many useful steps. The first of these is "self talk." It has been shown through extensive research, that self-talk for students who suffer from test anxiety, should be well monitored, in order to make sure that it contributes to self confidence as opposed to sinking the student. Frequently the self talk of test-anxious students is negative or self-defeating, thinking that everyone else is smarter and faster, that they always mess up, and that if they don't do well, they'll fail the entire course. It is important to decreasing anxiety that awareness is made of self talk. Try writing any negative self thoughts and then disputing them with a positive statement instead. Begin self-encouragement as though it was a friend speaking. Repeat positive statements to help reprogram the mind to believing in successes instead of failures.

Helpful Techniques

Other extremely helpful techniques include:

Self-visualization of doing well and reaching goals
While aiming for an "A" level of understanding, don't try to "overprotect" by setting your expectations lower. This will only convince the mind to stop studying in order to meet the lower expectations.
Don't make comparisons with the results or habits of other students. These are individual factors, and different things work for different people, causing different results.
Strive to become an expert in learning what works well, and what can be done in order to improve. Consider collecting this data in a journal.
Create rewards for after studying instead of doing things before studying that will only turn into avoidance behaviors.
Make a practice of relaxing - by using methods such as progressive relaxation, self-hypnosis, guided imagery, etc - in order to make relaxation an automatic sensation.
Work on creating a state of relaxed concentration so that concentrating will take on the focus of the mind, so that none will be wasted on worrying.
Take good care of the physical self by eating well and getting enough sleep.
Plan in time for exercise and stick to this plan.

Beyond these techniques, there are other methods to be used before, during and after the test that will help the test-taker perform well in addition to overcoming anxiety.

Before the exam comes the academic preparation. This involves establishing a study schedule and beginning at least one week before the actual date of the test. By doing this, the anxiety of not having enough time to study for the test will be automatically eliminated. Moreover, this will make the studying a much more effective experience, ensuring that the learning will be an easier process. This relieves much undue pressure on the test-taker.

Summary sheets, note cards, and flash cards with the main concepts and examples of these main concepts should be prepared in advance of the actual studying time. A topic should never be eliminated from this process. By omitting a topic because it isn't expected to be on the test is only setting up the test-taker for anxiety should it actually appear on the exam. Utilize the course syllabus for laying out the topics that should be studied. Carefully go over the notes that were made in class, paying special attention to any of the issues that the professor took special care to emphasize while lecturing in class. In the textbooks, use the chapter review, or if possible, the chapter tests, to begin your review.

It may even be possible to ask the instructor what information will be covered on the exam, or what the format of the exam will be (for example, multiple choice, essay, free form, true-false). Additionally, see if it is possible to find out how many questions will be on the test. If a review sheet or sample test has been offered by the professor, make good use of it, above anything else, for the preparation for the test. Another great resource for getting to know the examination is reviewing tests from previous semesters. Use these tests to review, and aim to achieve a 100% score on each of the possible topics. With a few exceptions, the goal that you set for yourself is the highest one that you will reach.

Take all of the questions that were assigned as homework, and rework them to any other possible course material. The more problems reworked, the more skill and confidence will form as a result. When forming the solution to a problem, write out each of the steps. Don't simply do head work. By doing as many steps on paper as possible, much clarification and therefore confidence will be formed. Do this with as many homework problems as possible, before checking the answers. By checking the answer after each problem, a reinforcement will exist, that will not be on the exam. Study situations should be as exam-like as possible, to prime the test-taker's system for the experience. By waiting to check the answers at the end, a psychological advantage will be formed, to decrease the stress factor.

Another fantastic reason for not cramming is the avoidance of confusion in concepts, especially when it comes to mathematics. 8-10 hours of study will become one hundred percent more effective if it is spread out over a week or at least several days, instead of doing it all in one sitting. Recognize that the human brain requires time in order to assimilate new material, so frequent breaks and a span of study time over several days will be much more beneficial.

Additionally, don't study right up until the point of the exam. Studying should stop a minimum of one hour before the exam begins. This allows the brain to rest and put things in their proper order. This will also provide the time to become as relaxed as possible when going into the examination room. The test-taker will also have time to eat well and eat sensibly. Know that the brain needs food as much as the rest of the body. With enough food and enough sleep, as well as a relaxed attitude, the body and the mind are primed for success.

Avoid any anxious classmates who are talking about the exam. These students only spread anxiety, and are not worth sharing the anxious sentimentalities.

Before the test also involves creating a positive attitude, so mental preparation should also be a point of concentration. There are many keys to creating a positive attitude. Should fears become rushing in, make a visualization of taking the exam, doing well, and seeing an A written on the paper. Write out a list of affirmations that will bring a feeling of confidence, such as "I am doing well in my English class," "I studied well and know my material," "I enjoy this class." Even if the affirmations aren't believed at first, it sends a positive message to the subconscious which will result in an alteration of the overall belief system, which is the system that creates reality.

If a sensation of panic begins, work with the fear and imagine the very worst! Work through the entire scenario of not passing the test, failing the entire course, and dropping out of school, followed by not getting a job, and pushing a shopping cart through the dark alley where you'll live. This will place things into perspective! Then, practice deep breathing and create a visualization of the opposite situation - achieving an "A" on the exam, passing the entire course, receiving the degree at a graduation ceremony.

On the day of the test, there are many things to be done to ensure the best results, as well as the most calm outlook. The following stages are suggested in order to maximize test-taking potential:

Begin the examination day with a moderate breakfast, and avoid any coffee or beverages with caffeine if the test taker is prone to jitters. Even people who are used to managing caffeine can feel jittery or light-headed when it is taken on a test day.
Attempt to do something that is relaxing before the examination begins. As last minute cramming clouds the mastering of overall concepts, it is better to use this time to create a calming outlook.
Be certain to arrive at the test location well in advance, in order to provide time to select a location that is away from doors, windows and other distractions, as well as giving enough time to relax before the test begins.
Keep away from anxiety generating classmates who will upset the sensation of stability and relaxation that is being attempted before the exam.
Should the waiting period before the exam begins cause anxiety, create a self-distraction by reading a light magazine or something else that is relaxing and simple.

During the exam itself, read the entire exam from beginning to end, and find out how much time should be allotted to each individual problem. Once writing the exam, should more time be taken for a problem, it should be abandoned, in order to begin another problem. If there is time at the end, the unfinished problem can always be returned to and completed.

Read the instructions very carefully - twice - so that unpleasant surprises won't follow during or after the exam has ended.

When writing the exam, pretend that the situation is actually simply the completion of homework within a library, or at home. This will assist in forming a relaxed atmosphere, and will allow the brain extra focus for the complex thinking function.

Begin the exam with all of the questions with which the most confidence is felt. This will build the confidence level regarding the entire exam and will begin a quality momentum. This will also create encouragement for trying the problems where uncertainty resides.

Going with the "gut instinct" is always the way to go when solving a problem. Second guessing should be avoided at all costs. Have confidence in the ability to do well.

For essay questions, create an outline in advance that will keep the mind organized and make certain that all of the points are remembered. For multiple choice, read every answer, even if the correct one has been spotted - a better one may exist.

Continue at a pace that is reasonable and not rushed, in order to be able to work carefully. Provide enough time to go over the answers at the end, to check for small errors that can be corrected.

Should a feeling of panic begin, breathe deeply, and think of the feeling of the body releasing sand through its pores. Visualize a calm, peaceful place, and include all of the sights, sounds and sensations of this image. Continue the deep breathing, and take a few minutes to continue this with closed eyes. When all is well again, return to the test.

If a "blanking" occurs for a certain question, skip it and move on to the next question. There will be time to return to the other question later. Get everything done that can be done, first, to guarantee all the grades that can be compiled, and to build all of the confidence possible. Then return to the weaker questions to build the marks from there.

Remember, one's own reality can be created, so as long as the belief is there, success will follow. And remember: anxiety can happen later, right now, there's an exam to be written!

After the examination is complete, whether there is a feeling for a good grade or a bad grade, don't dwell on the exam, and be certain to follow through on the reward that was promised...and enjoy it! Don't dwell on any mistakes that have been made, as there is nothing that can be done at this point anyway.

Additionally, don't begin to study for the next test right away. Do something relaxing for a while, and let the mind relax and prepare itself to begin absorbing information again.

From the results of the exam - both the grade and the entire experience, be certain to learn from what has gone on. Perfect studying habits and work some more on confidence in order to make the next examination experience even better than the last one.

Learn to avoid places where openings occurred for laziness, procrastination and day dreaming.

Use the time between this exam and the next one to better learn to relax, even learning to relax on cue, so that any anxiety can be controlled during the next exam. Learn how to relax the body. Slouch in your chair if that helps. Tighten and then relax all of the different muscle groups, one group at a time, beginning with the feet and then working all the way up to the neck and face. This will ultimately relax the muscles more than they were to begin with. Learn how to breathe deeply and comfortably, and focus on this breathing going in and out as a relaxing thought. With every exhale, repeat the word "relax."

As common as test anxiety is, it is very possible to overcome it. Make yourself one of the test-takers who overcome this frustrating hindrance.

Special Report: Additional Bonus Material

Due to our efforts to try to keep this book to a manageable length, we've created a link that will give you access to all of your additional bonus material.

Please visit http://www.mometrix.com/bonus948/pectspedprek8 to access the information.